New England
A PHOTOGRAPHIC PORTRAIT

PHOTOGRAPHY BY

Tom Croke

NARRATIVE BY

Sara Day

TWIN LIGHTS PUBLISHERS, ROCKPORT, MASSACHUSETTS

Copyright © 2014 by
Twin Lights Publishers, Inc.

All rights reserved. No part of this book may be reproduced in any form without written permission of the copyright owners. All images in this book have been reproduced with the knowledge and prior consent of the artists concerned and no responsibility is accepted by producer, publisher, or printer for any infringement of copyright or otherwise, arising from the contents of this publication. Every effort has been made to ensure that credits accurately comply with information supplied.

First published in the United States of America by:

Twin Lights Publishers, Inc.
51 Broadway
Rockport, Massachusetts 01966
Telephone: (978) 546-7398
www.twinlightspub.com

ISBN: 978-1-934907-17-7

10 9 8 7 6 5 4 3 2 1

(*opposite*)
Salt Marsh, West Harwich, MA

(*frontispiece*)
The Windjammer *American Eagle*, Rockland, ME

(*jacket front*)
Gilbert Stuart Birthplace & Museum, Saunderstown, RI

(*jacket back*)
Portland Head Light, Cape Elizabeth, ME
Maple Sugaring, Moretown, VT

Book design by:
SYP Design & Production, Inc.
www.sypdesign.com

Printed in China

New England is a place well known for magnificent coastlines and inspirational mountain ranges, but the details that define this incredible place are as vast as the Atlantic is blue. New England is a keeper of American history, of family traditions, and succulent secret recipes. It can steal the hearts of lifelong residents and visitors alike by transforming turbulent weather into sheer art. From crystal clear streams that flow down a Vermont mountainside during a spring thaw, to the cool brisk air that fills a Cape Cod sail in summer; from that first crisp bite of an apple from a local orchard in autumn, to the soothing quiet of the first winter snowfall that gently blankets gold and amber leaves, New England is a place that moves the spirit and refreshes the soul.

New Englanders are a hardy bunch who guard the beauty and integrity of this place with great pride and an open door to all who come to experience this region. Deep roots that have spawned excellence in agriculture, education, and innovation have greatly contributed to America's growth and core principles. And although they don't like to brag, a native New Englander is truly a seasoned professor in one of the world's most amazing classrooms.

The earliest settlers quickly discovered that the northeast Atlantic environment provides rich agricultural resources, and through the years, generations of farmers and innovators have created companies like Birds Eye and OceanSpray, that have contributed much to the region's economy. From cranberries, to maple syrup, to fresh Atlantic seafood, these resources continue to create endless opportunities.

Some of the world's most sought-out colleges and universities are rooted in New England. It is considered the center of continuing education in the fields of medicine, law, technology, finance, art, architecture, literature, and more. And New England's innumerable galleries and museums surely hold testimony of how the striking beauty of these surroundings has inspired so many famous artists such as Winslow Homer, Frank Weston Benson, and Edward Hopper, among others.

One visit wouldn't be nearly enough to experience the multi-colored personalities of these six exquisitely unique states. Throughout these pages, photographer Tom Croke has vividly captured the essence of each and every one.

Nauset Light (*opposite*)
EASTHAM, MA

One of the most photographed structures on Cape Cod, the 48-foot-tall Nauset Light was built in 1877 and replaced three smaller wood structures called the *Three Sisters of Nauset*. Often recognized as the logo for Cape Cod Potato Chips, it was rescued from an eroding cliff in 1996 and moved 300 feet to its present location.

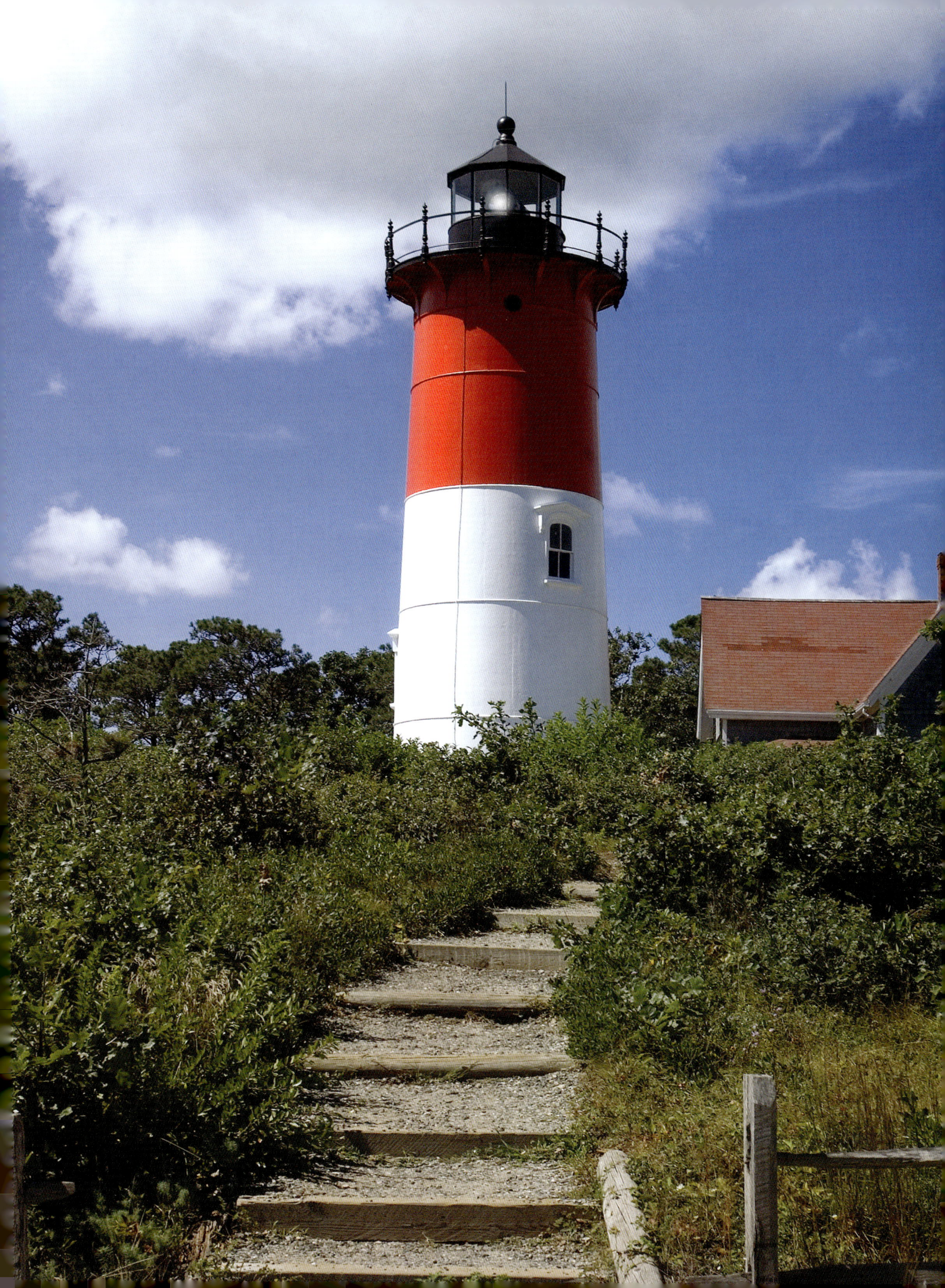

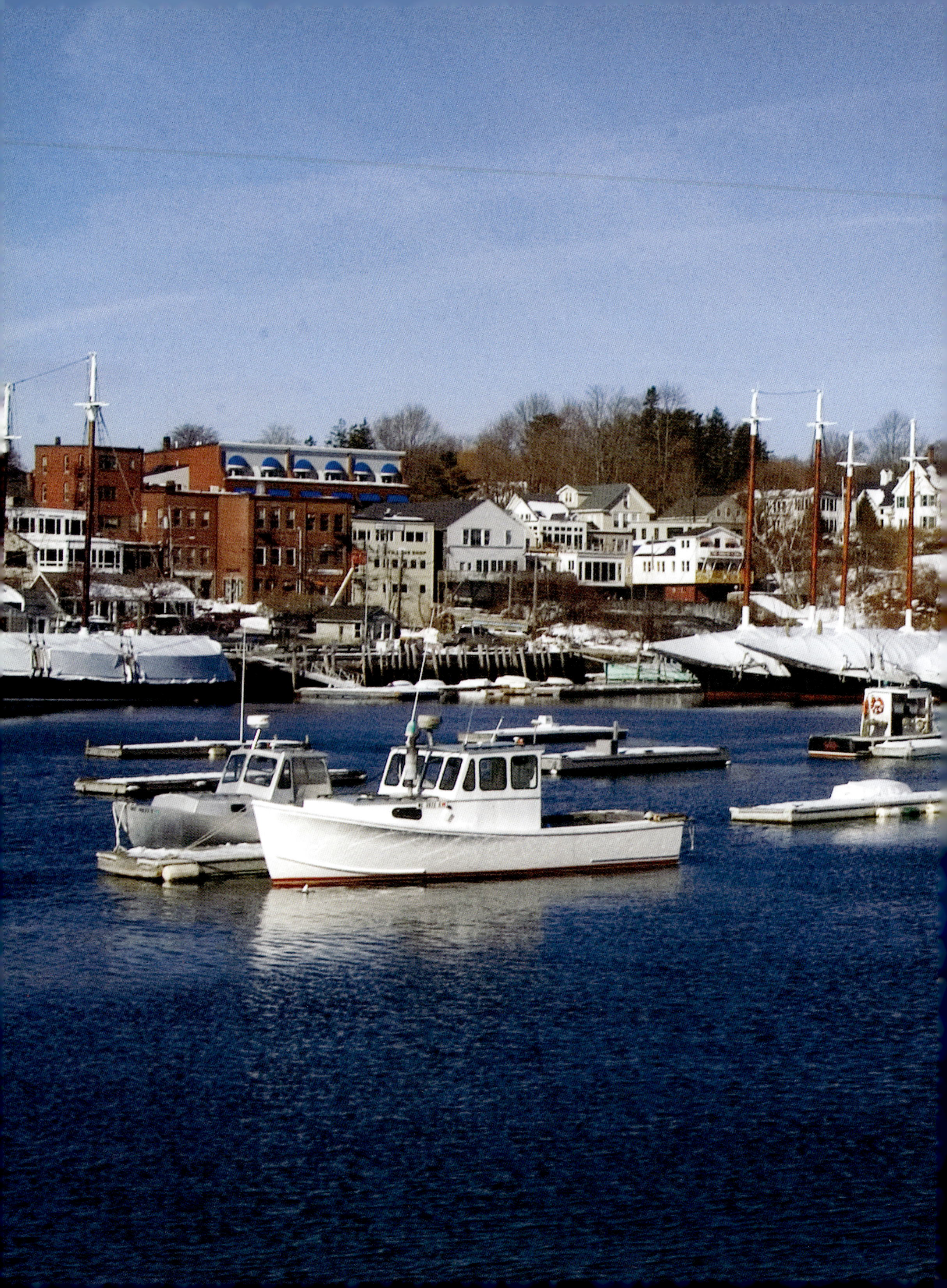

Maine

The Pine Tree State

CAMDEN HARBOR, CAMDEN, ME

8 MAINE

Bass Harbor Head Light *(opposite)*
MOUNT DESERT ISLAND, ME

Marking the entrance to Bass Harbor in Tremont, Bass Harbor Head Light, built in 1858, adorns the rugged cliffs of Acadia National Park on the southwestern side of Mount Desert Island. Only the grounds are open to the public and include paths to panoramic harbor views. It is listed on the National Register of Historic Places.

Balance Rock, Acadia National Park *(top)*
BAR HARBOR, ME

Perched precariously atop South Bubble is Balance Rock, also known as Bubble Rock. The huge bolder, or "glacial erratic," is unlike its surrounding rocky platform, having been set there by a glacier ages ago. North and South Bubble Mountains are popular hiking spots, offering breathtaking vistas of Jordan Pond and beyond.

Early Autumn *(bottom)*
SOMESVILLE, ME

Early autumn strikes a pose and reflects a hint of imminent winter in the waters of Somes Sound. Settled in 1761, Somesville was the first village established on Mount Desert Island. Coves, inlets, and beautiful mountain views, whose colors mark the season, make this a wonderful place to explore, any time of year.

Stonington Harbor
STONINGTON, ME

The remnants of a New England sunset cast a warm glow over lobster boats in picturesque Stonington Harbor. Deer Isle and Stonington are beautiful island communities on Penobscot Bay that draw tourists, artists, and nature lovers who enjoy tranquil coves, historic lighthouses, and exquisite seafood.

Pemaquid Point Light Station (top)
BRISTOL, ME

High atop a veil of cascading granite, the Pemaquid Point Light navigates ships off the coast of Bristol with a beacon that can be seen for 14 nautical miles. First built in 1827, it was upgraded with a more solid structure in 1835. The lighthouse park features a Fisherman's Museum, art gallery, learning center, as well as picnic areas.

Camden Harbor (bottom)
CAMDEN, ME

From classic windjammers to working watercraft, an array of boats rest in the safety of Camden Harbor. The quaint New England town *'where the mountains meet the sea'* was settled in 1791 and epitomizes the spirit of coastal Maine with a hilly and mountainous landscape that surrounds a quiet harbor.

MAINE 11

Whaleback Light *(above)*
KITTERY, ME

Accessible only by boat, Whaleback Light is located at the mouth of the Piscataqua River, south of Wood Island. The original tower, established in 1820, yielded to storm damage and was eventually dismantled. The existing 50-foot-tall granite structure was built in 1872 and is listed on the National Register of Historic Places.

Lobstering *(opposite, top)*
BOOTHBAY HARBOR, ME

No matter what the weather, Maine lobstermen harvest millions of pounds of this delectable crustacean each year. The eco-friendly industry has sustained itself for generations due to adaptable government regulations on traps and size limits and the good common sense of these experienced, hard-working harvesters.

Burnt Island Light *(opposite, bottom)*
BOOTHBAY HARBOR, ME

Burnt Island Light was transformed into a living history museum by the Maine Department of Marine Resources in 2003. Here, school children can explore the island's five acres of rocky shores and dense forest, while interpreters in period costume enlighten guests with 1950s Maine maritime history.

MAINE 13

Owl's Head Light *(top)*
OWL'S HEAD, ME

Construction of the 30-foot-tall Owl's Head Light was authorized by President John Quincy Adams in 1825. Included on *Coastal Living* magazine's most haunted lighthouse list, it has a history of mysterious events. Located at the mouth of Rockland Harbor, it is managed by the Friends of the Rockland Breakwater Lighthouse.

Portland Head Light *(bottom)*
CAPE ELIZABETH, ME

Cape Elizabeth boasts one of Maine's most famous landmarks—Portland Head Light, which was first lit with 16 whale oil lamps in 1791. The former Keepers' Quarters is now home to an award-winning museum where visitors can view lighthouse displays and roam the grounds of historic Fort Williams Park.

Fort McClary
KITTERY POINT, ME

Built in 1808 to guard the entrance to the Piscataqua River, Fort McClary was named for New Hampshire native, Major Andrew McClary. It is the second military fortress to occupy the site since 1689. The hexagonal blockhouse, built in 1884, is the last of its kind to be built in Maine and now serves as a museum.

Coastal Maine Botanical Gardens
BOOTHBAY, ME

Blooming along Maine's glistening coastline are 250 acres of natural wonder to explore. Coastal Maine Botanical Gardens is enchantingly comprised of formal gardens, waterfalls, and antique stone walls. Horticultural experts offer free tours along groomed trails after which visitors can enjoy a bite at the Kitchen Garden Café.

Horticultural Heaven
BOOTHBAY, ME

Stone paths meander through colorful cascading flora in the horticultural heaven that is Coastal Maine Botanical Gardens, where visitors can explore year round. In keeping with technology, the gardens feature FloraFind, an online searchable database where you can identify plants and take virtual garden tours.

MAINE 17

Gathering Hay

THOMASTON, ME

Bales of freshly mowed hay are gathered in Thomaston, a quaint gem of mid-coastal Maine. This seaport town is well known for its antique architecture as well as Montpelier, an elegant museum on the St. Georges River, once the home of Revolutionary General Henry Knox. The estate, built in 1795, is now open to the public.

Boothbay Railway Village *(top)*
BOOTHBAY, ME

Vintage transportation buffs flock to Boothbay Railway Village to experience authentic railroad history. Steam locomotives make their way through the village on an over three-quarters of a mile track. The museum includes authentic railroad stations, antique automobiles, and historic buildings that take visitors back in time to experience lifestyles during the mid-1800s.

Great Blue Heron *(right)*
BOOTHBAY, ME

An unfortunate amphibian becomes a tasty snack for this Great Blue Heron along one of many pristine waterways found in Boothbay. A common sight on salt marshes and beaches, many of these graceful birds migrate south in winter, but in areas where there is plenty of open water, some may opt for a longer stay.

MAINE 19

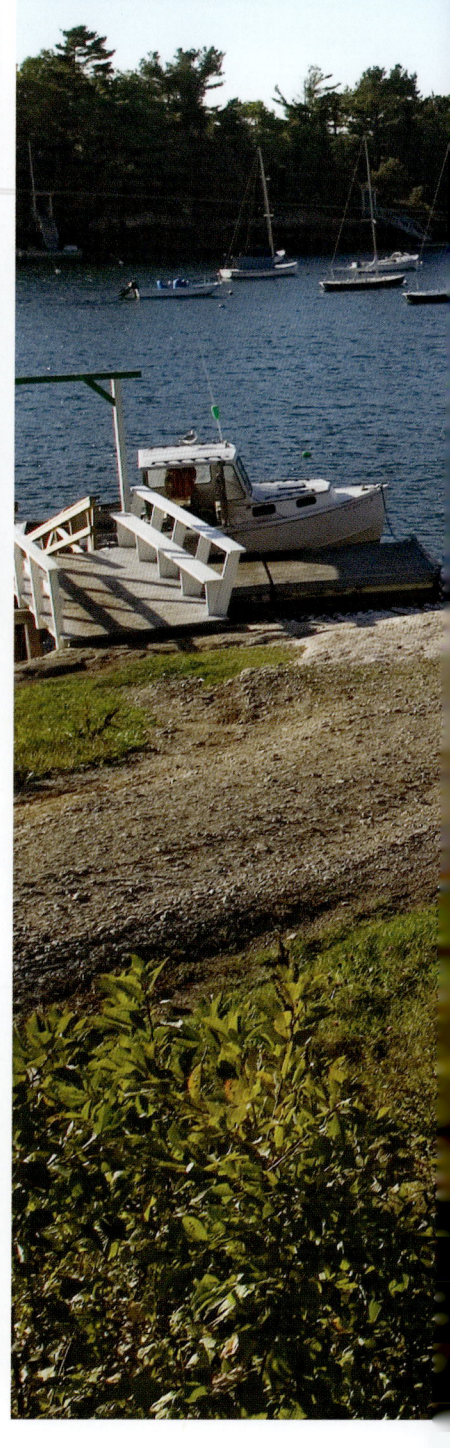

Autumn *(top)*
SOMESVILLE, ME

The graceful bow of a footbridge in a gentle autumn rain evokes the musings of writer and naturalist, Rachel Carson: "In autumn, oak and maple and birch set up a blaze of color that flamed and flickered across a backdrop of pines."
— from *Silent Spring*

Island Fog *(bottom)*
MONHEGAN ISLAND, ME

Unchanged, unpaved, and only accessible by boat, Monhegan Island is a remote haven for those fond of an easier pace. Located approximately ten miles off the coast of Maine in Lincoln County, the tiny seaport island, with an area of just one square mile, attracts summer artists, seafarers, and nature lovers alike.

Cozy Harbor
SOUTHPORT ISLAND, ME

Lobster traps lay stacked beside a weathered shanty at Cozy Harbor on Southport Island at the entrance of Sheepscot River. Accessible by swing bridge, the charming island is a favorite of summer vacationers who enjoy boating on sparkling waters and dining on only the freshest lobster, shrimp, and oysters.

JOSHUA L CHAMBERLAIN
1828 — 1914

Joshua Chamberlain Monument (opposite)
BRUNSWICK, ME

Civil War General Joshua Chamberlain led Union troops at the Battle of Gettysburg, yet he was best known for accepting the Confederacy's surrender at Appomattox, Virginia in 1865. Chamberlain served as Maine's Governor as well as President of Bowdoin College, where his bronze tribute stands today.

Cape Newagen (top)
SOUTHPORT, ME

Like a golden, unkempt mane, seaweed drapes the stones at low tide along Cape Newagen in Southport, artfully defining the topography. The Boothbay Harbor region, with its many islands, hidden coves, lighthouses, and Downeast hospitality is a perfect place to hike, boat, explore, or just unwind.

Fort Foster Beach (bottom)
KITTERY POINT, ME

Children discover sea life in tidal pools along the shores of the Piscataqua River on Fort Foster Beach. A manned fortress during World War II, the area includes trails and military relics. The now abandoned life-saving station in the background was built in the early 1900s and served as a rescue post for ships in peril.

You *Can* Get There From Here *(top)*
PORTLAND, ME

The islands of Casco Bay are popular tourist destinations, and water taxis and ferry boats make 'getting there' a wonderful part of the adventure. Scenic cruises to destinations such as Peaks Island, Diamond Pass, or Bailey Island offer glimpses of historic lighthouses, charming coastal cottages, as well as breathtaking ocean vistas.

Fryeburg Fair *(bottom)*
FRYEBURG, ME

Maine's oldest and largest agricultural event, the Fryeburg Fair has been celebrating the best of the regions produce, cattle, and crafts since 1851. Each year, in early October, people flock to the foothills of the White Mountains during this 8-day, fun-filled event to enjoy games, rides, and the largest livestock exhibit in the world.

Portland Waterfront *(opposite)*
PORTLAND, ME

With upscale condominiums, markets, and ferry docks, Portland's vibrant working waterfront thrives in summer. Visitors and residents alike take advantage of the season, enjoying whale-watch excursions or sunset cruises among the many islands in Casco Bay.

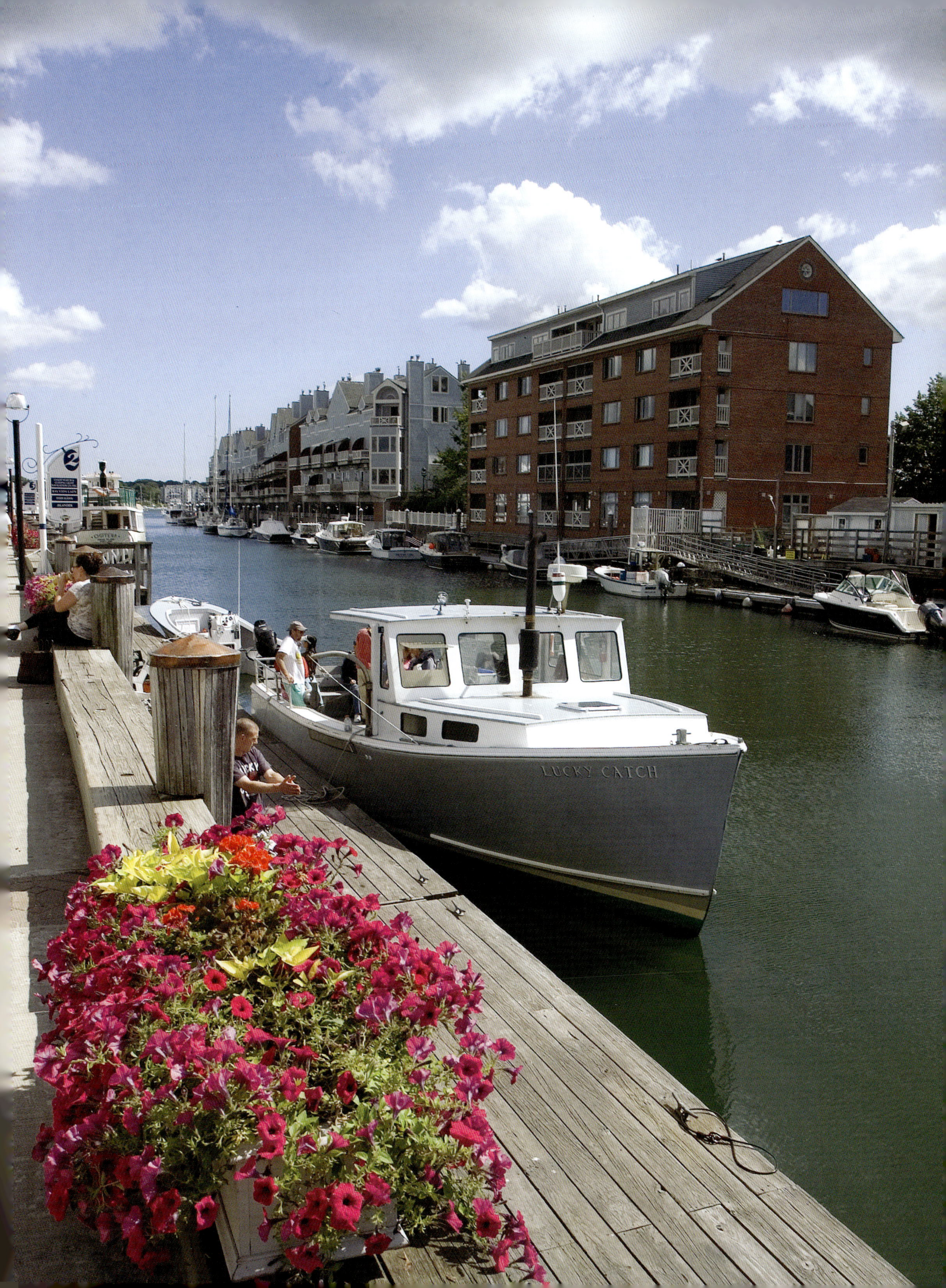
LUCKY CATCH

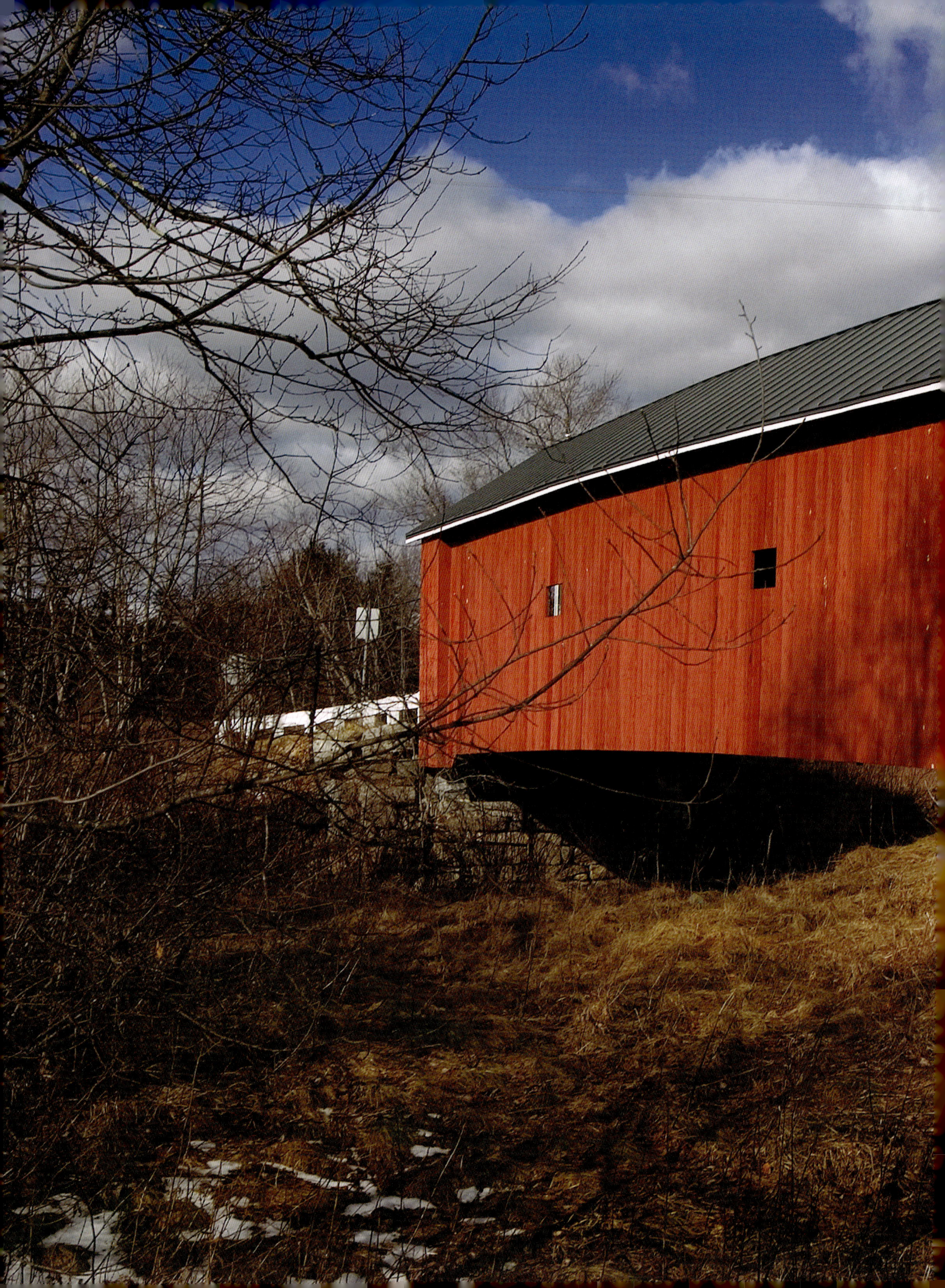

New Hampshire

The Granite State

CARLTON COVERED BRIDGE, SWANZEY, NH

FRANKLIN PIERCE

Statue of Franklin Pierce *(opposite)*
CONCORD, NH

Franklin Pierce, the 14th President of the United States, and the only President from New Hampshire, is memorialized in bronze on the grounds of the State Capitol in Concord. His unpopular views on slavery during the Civil War deemed his presidency controversial. Pierce is buried in the Old North Cemetery in Concord.

New Hampshire State Capitol *(top)*
CONCORD, NH

Built between 1816 and 1819, the New Hampshire State Capitol Building was designed in the Greek Revival style by architect Stuart Park. Located on North Main Street, the historic building houses the office of the Governor, the New Hampshire General Court, and the Executive Council.

Jaffrey Center Historic District *(bottom)*
JAFFREY, NH

The Jaffrey Meeting House was raised in 1775, the same day as the Battle of Bunker Hill. It has been used as a place of worship and as a town hall. The Little Red Schoolhouse (*left*) was built in 1822 and moved to this location in 1960. The one-room schoolhouse, with its authentic benches and books, is open to the public in summer.

Lake Winnipesaukee (top)
LACONIA, NH

With a perimeter of 182 miles, Lake Winnipesaukee is New Hampshire's largest fresh-water lake. Making the most of every square mile, the *Mount Washington* makes stops in five ports and offers daytime and sunset cruises, where visitors can enjoy beautiful mountain views as well as some of the lake's 258 islands.

Hampton Beach (bottom)
HAMPTON BEACH, NH

One of New England's most popular summer vacation spots, Hampton Beach offers sun, sand, and plenty of entertainment. Penny arcades, fried dough, and souvenir shops that line Ocean Boulevard add to the area's unique vibrancy. Visitors enjoy headline shows at the Casino Ballroom and a fabulous weekly fireworks display.

Center Meeting House (opposite)
NEWBURY, NH

Built with fine craftsmanship in 1832, this Federal-style meeting house was designed by architect, Asher Benjamin. Its rarest feature is the reverse pulpit design where parishioners face toward the entrance. Researchers suggest the reason being is that no part of the building would be regarded as more sacred than another.

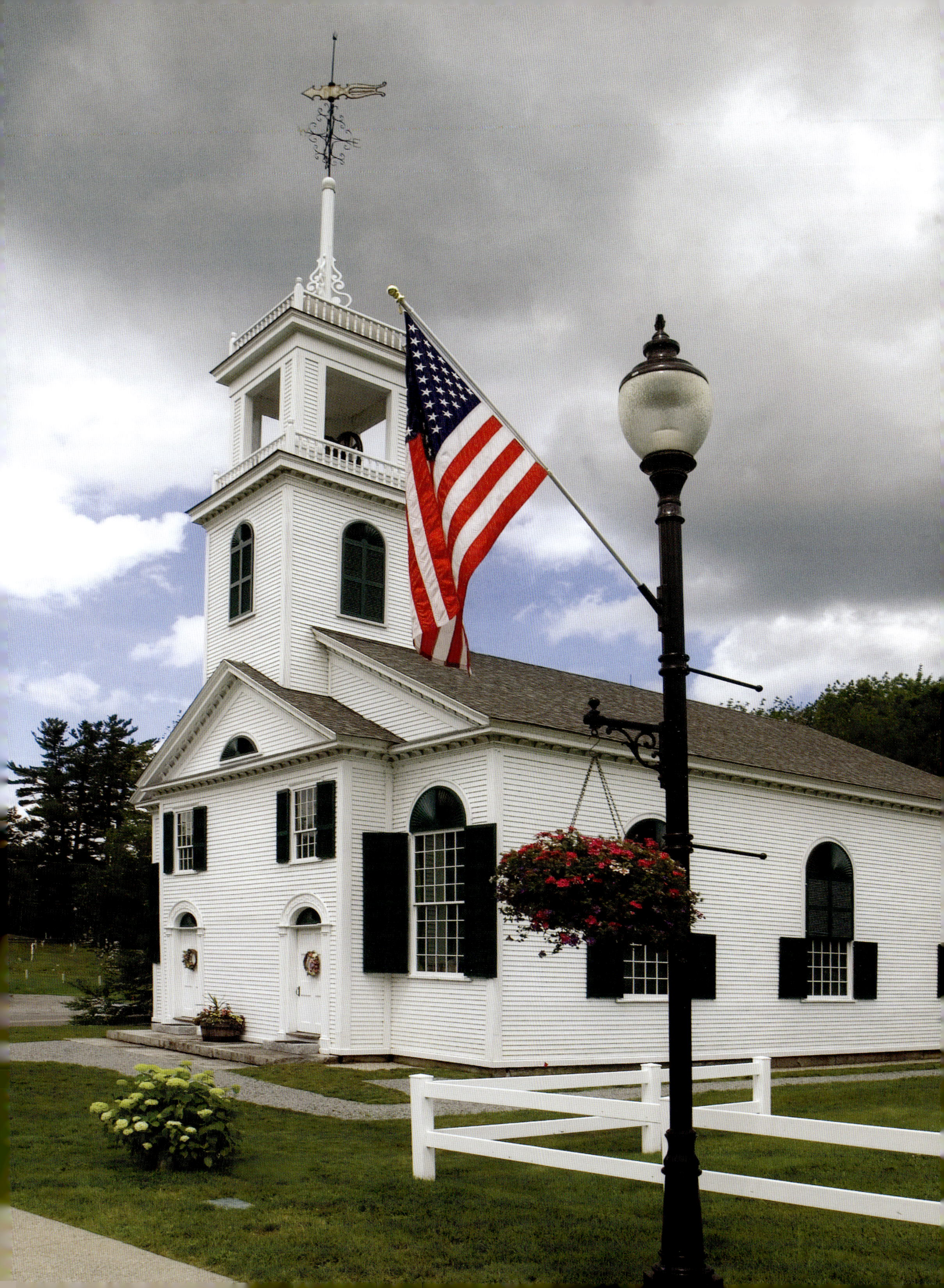

All Aboard! *(top)*
WEIRS BEACH, NH

Passengers board the Winnipesaukee Scenic Railroad at the Weirs Beach station for an excursion along the shores of New Hampshire's largest lake. Built in 1849, the railway travels from Meredith to Weirs Beach, offering stunning views. Together with the Hobo Railroad, these historic trains are a treasured part of White Mountains lore.

Canterbury Shaker Village *(bottom)*
CANTERBURY, NH

Canterbury Shaker Village preserves the heritage of Shaker life through education, exhibits, and more. Founded in 1792, it had grown to include nearly 100 buildings. Today, this National Historic Landmark is comprised of 25 original Shaker buildings, including a school house, a meeting house, a barn, and an infirmary.

Warm Welcome *(opposite)*
LITTLETON, NH

Forever cheerful, the fictional *Pollyanna* extends a warm welcome from the library in downtown Littleton. Littleton was the birthplace of author Eleanor Hodgman Porter, creator of the novels that featured the highly optimistic orphan girl who would eventually become the personification of gladness itself.

POLLYANNA

White Mountains
WHITE MOUNTAINS, NH

Some of New England's most breathtaking splendor can be found along the White Mountains scenic byways. Widely traveled trails include the Northern Loop, the Southern Loop, and the National Scenic Byway. The Presidential Range features the 6,288-foot Mount Washington, known for its incredible vistas and extreme weather.

Cannon Mountain Aerial Tramway
FRANCONIA, NH

From May to October, eager spectators aboard the Aerial Tramway ascend 4,080 feet to the summit of Cannon Mountain. The thrilling 10-minute ride is only part of the adventure. At the summit, on a clear day, visitors are able to enjoy panoramic views of Maine, New Hampshire, Vermont, New York, and Canada.

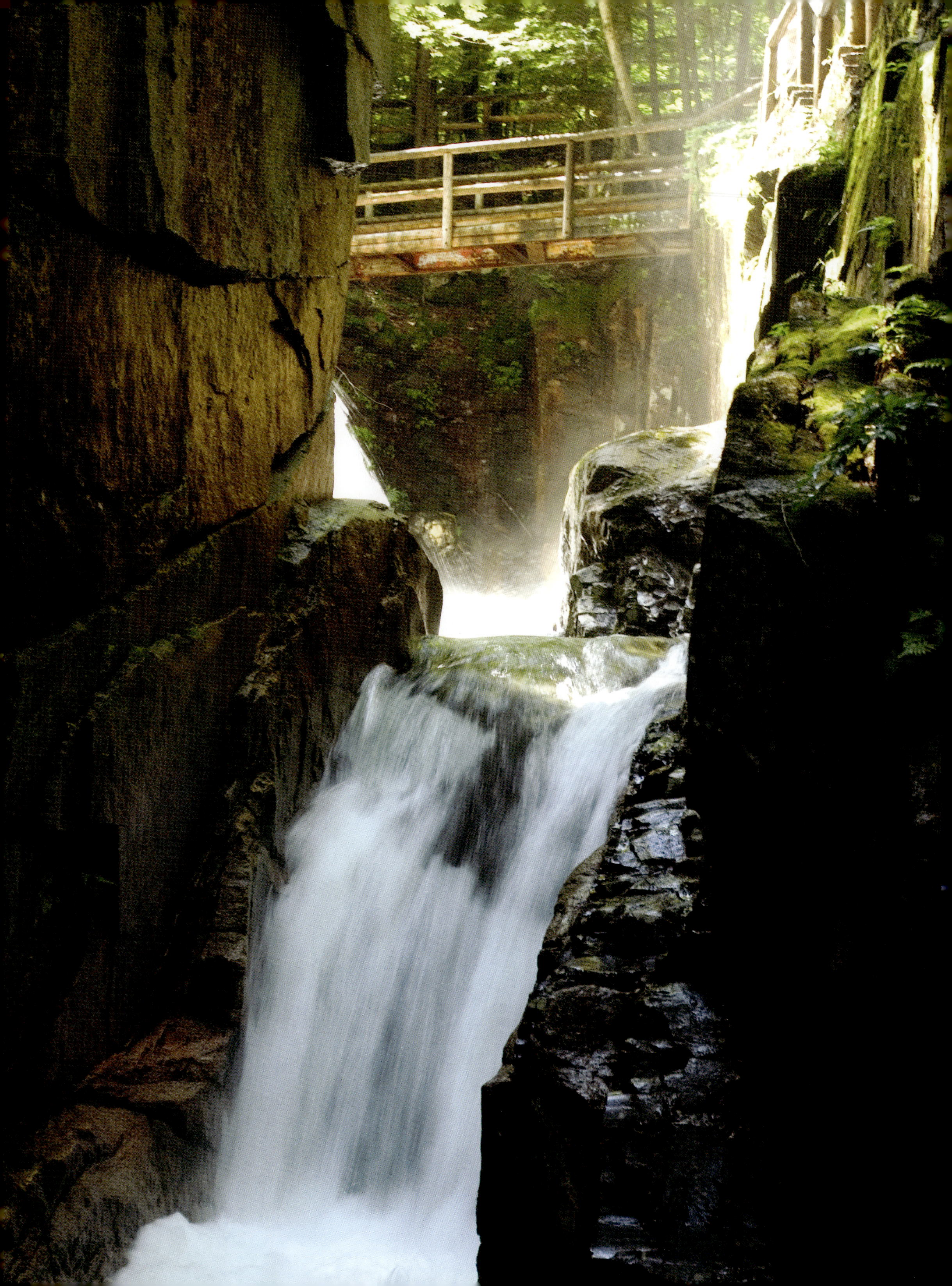

Sabbaday Falls (opposite)
WATERVILLE, NH

A prime example of the natural splendor found in the White Mountains National Forest is Sabbaday Falls in Waterville, just off the Kancamagus Scenic Byway. A short hike leads to a variety of observation areas where the upper and middle falls cascade into the lower falls that, in turn, pour into a crystal clear pool.

New England Zen (top)
FRANCONIA, NH

A fly fisherman gracefully casts his line out into calm waters at Franconia Notch State Park. Recreation—including fishing, biking, hiking, rock climbing, and bird watching—coupled with some of the most beautiful scenery in the region, draws thousands of visitors to Franconia every year.

White Water Adventure (bottom)
LINCOLN, NH

Rapids along the Pemigewasset River are a welcome challenge for three adventurous kayakers in Lincoln. Whether paddling river rapids, canoeing on still lakes, or enjoying a sea kayaking adventure, the Granite State offers outstanding water recreation that is second to none.

NEW HAMPSHIRE 37

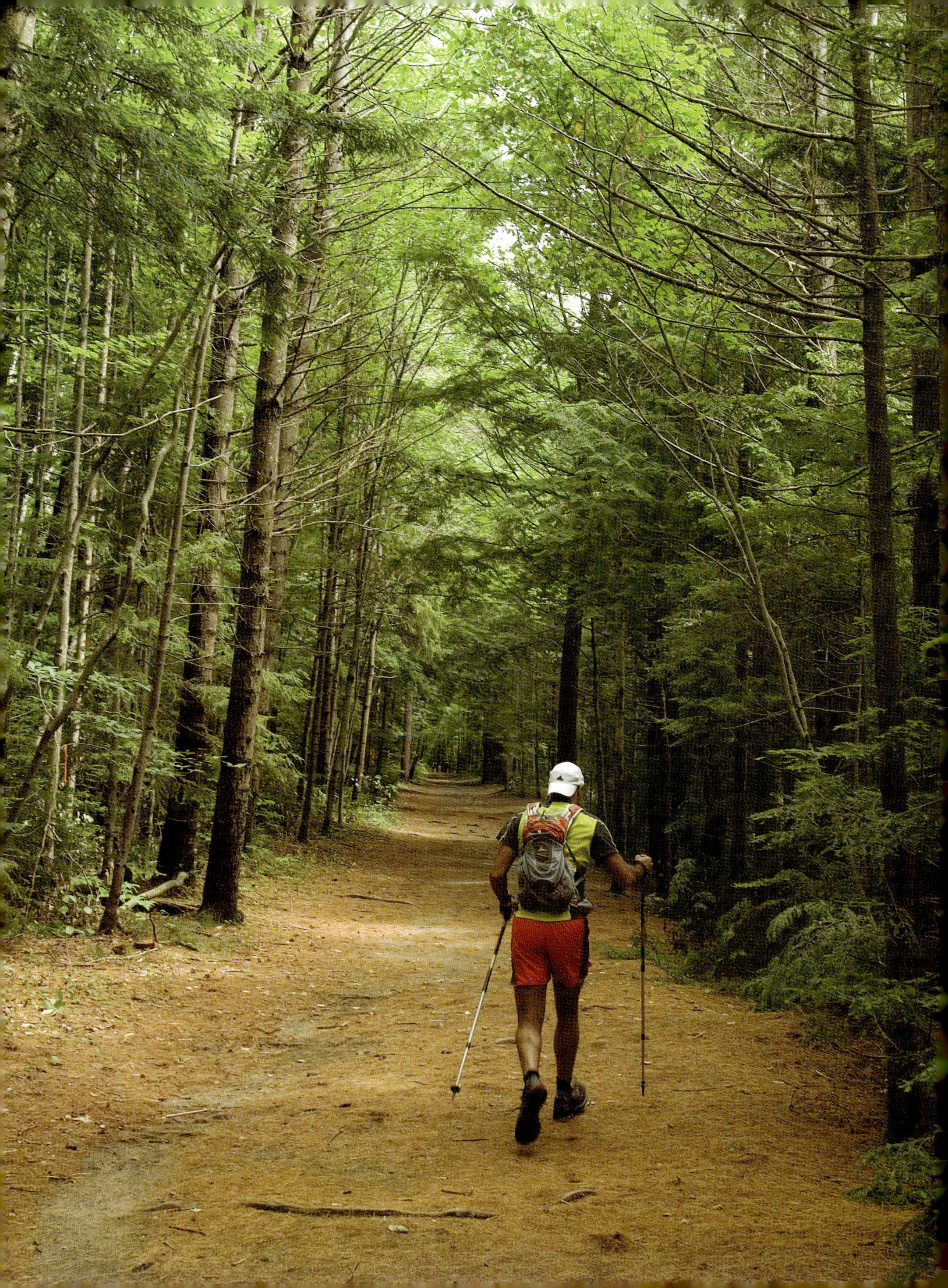

Woodland Adventure *(opposite)*
LINCOLN, NH

Whether day hiking or weekend camping, Lincoln Woods offers the ultimate woodland adventure. Cool and inviting, the Lincoln Woods Trail, located on the Kancamagus Highway, connects with other trails that lead nature lovers to beautiful ponds, cascading falls, and breathtaking mountain views.

Oracle House *(top)*
PORTSMOUTH, NH

Built circa 1702 by British Royal Navy officer and wealthy merchant, Richard Wibird, the Oracle House has the distinction of being one of the oldest houses in New England. It was here, during the 18th century, that the first daily newspaper in New Hampshire was published—*The Oracle of the Day*.

Prescott Park *(bottom)*
PORTSMOUTH, NH

Along the banks of the Piscataqua River in Portsmouth is Prescott Park—ten acres of beautiful gardens, walking paths, fountains, and waterfront lawns. Those arriving by boat have access to one of two public docking areas. The park is managed by the Trustees of Trust Funds of the City of Portsmouth.

NEW HAMPSHIRE 39

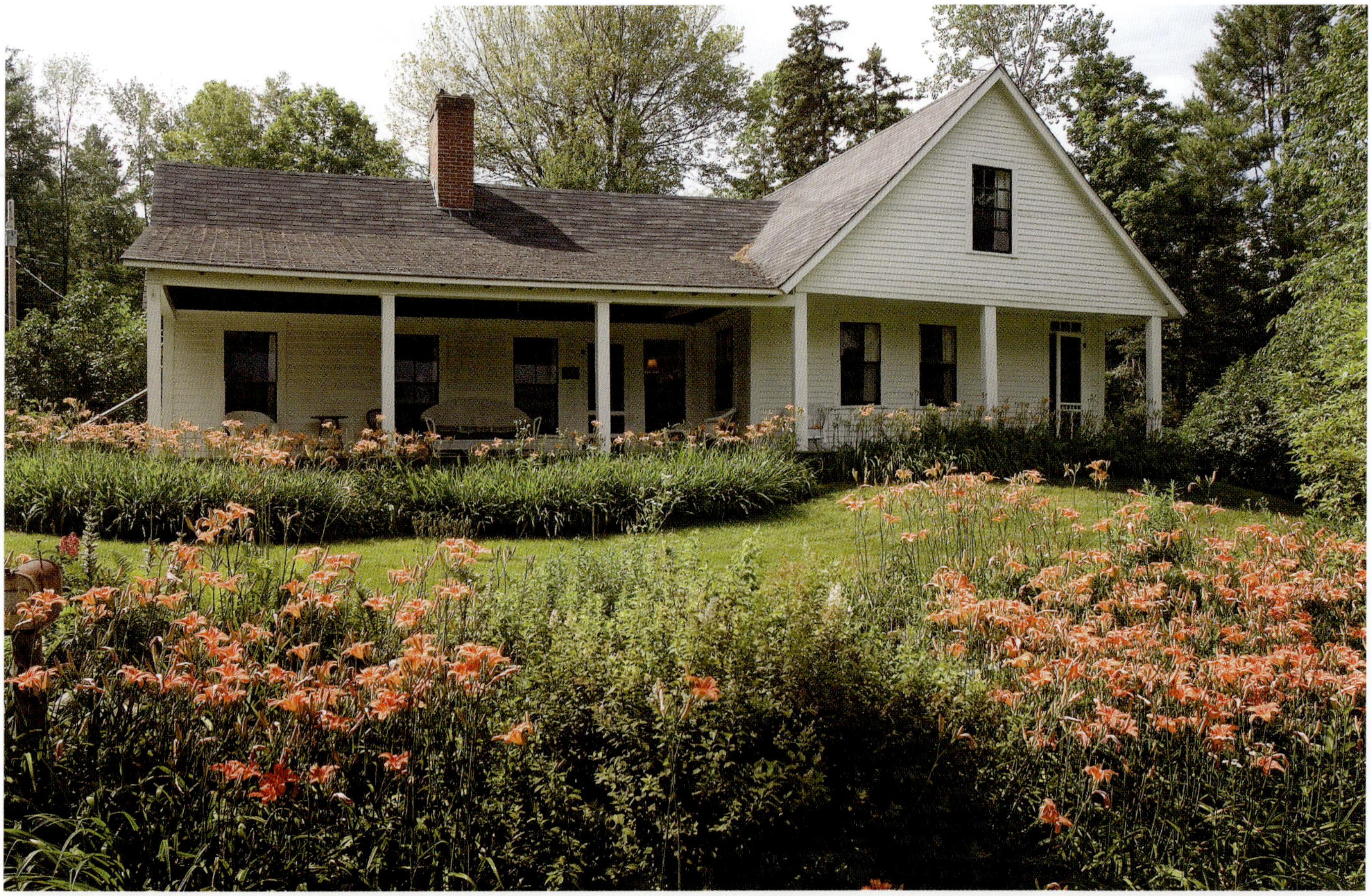

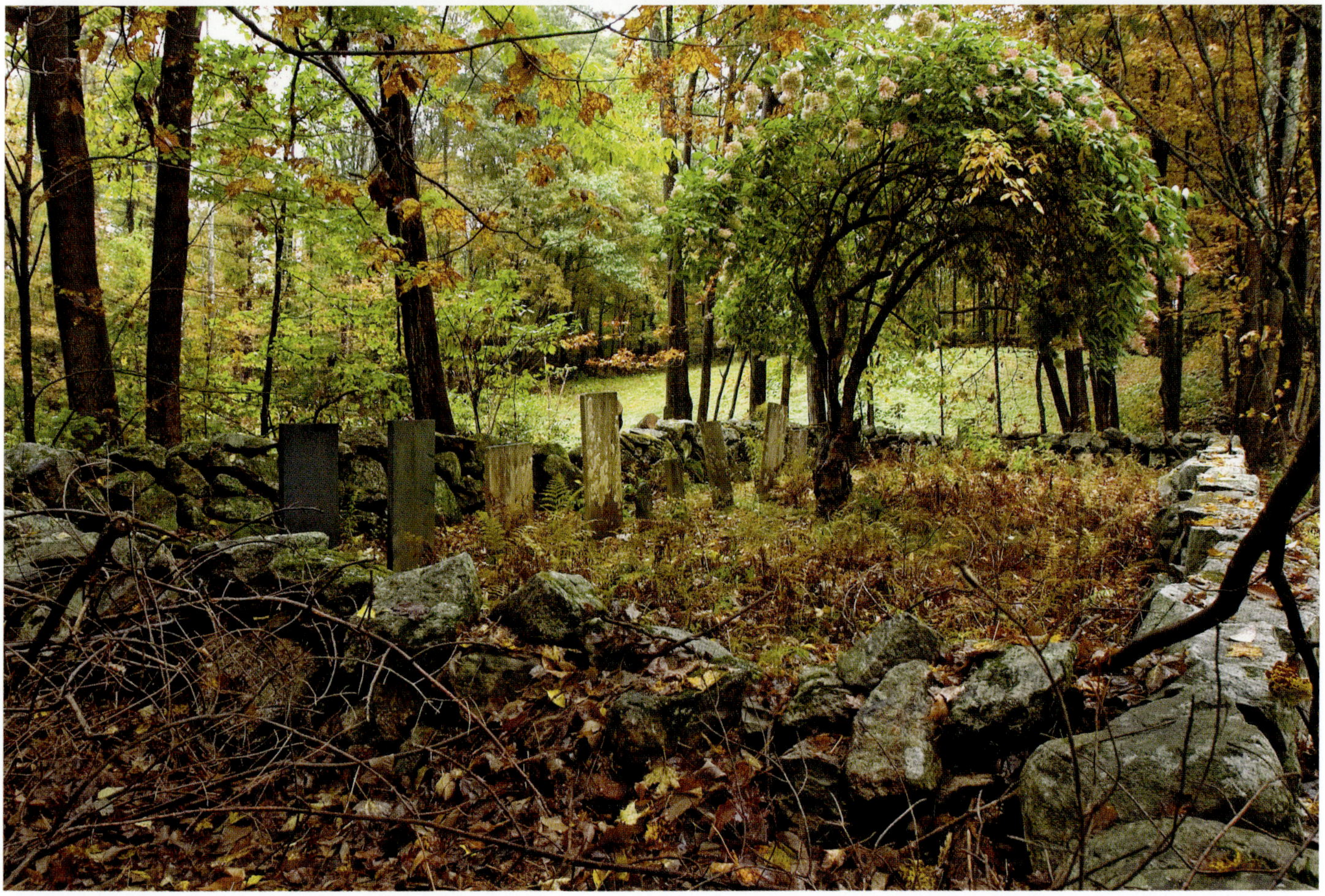

The Frost Place *(opposite, top)*
FRANCONIA, NH

In 1915, American poet Robert Frost moved his family into this 1860's farmhouse in Franconia. Today, the home, with its spectacular views of the White Mountains, is a museum for poetry enthusiasts and those who would appreciate a glimpse of the quaint and modest surroundings that inspired Frost's great works.

Old Graveyard *(opposite, bottom)*
CANTERBURY, NH

Tilted slabs of granite, slate, and limestone stand as historical markers that tell the stories of New Englanders past. The New Hampshire Old Graveyard Association, with the help of historians and genealogists, is developing a searchable database, collecting invaluable information on centuries-old New Hampshire burials.

Canterbury Charm *(above)*
CANTERBURY, NH

As if posing for a Currier and Ives illustration, a farm wagon sits in a Canterbury field—its simplicity overshadowed by its bright yellow wheels. Although heartfully appreciated, locals may sometimes take picturesque scenes like this for granted, yet these quintessential vignettes draw thousands of visitors to the area each year.

Lake Sunapee *(top)*
NEWBURY, NH

Surrounded by the towns of Sunapee, New London, and Newbury, the crystal waters of Lake Sunapee offer year-round recreation. From sailing in summer, to ice fishing in winter, the long narrow lake is dotted with eight islands and has three lighthouses that are included on the National Register of Historic Places.

Colonel Benjamin Prescott Inn *(bottom)*
JAFFREY, NH

Built in 1853 by Revolutionary Colonel Benjamin Prescott, one of Jaffrey's first settlers, this 23-room Greek Revival-style inn is surrounded by acres of stunningly unspoiled scenery. The inn's charming rooms, each named for a Prescott family member, are tastefully decorated with period furnishings.

Lake Sunapee *(above)*
NEWBURY, NH

An antique service station along the shores of Lake Sunapee smacks of a simpler by-gone era and is evidence of the relaxing, small-town feel of this much-visited vacation spot. With several sandy beaches to enjoy in summer, and plenty of skiing in winter, it's a region that invites you to unplug and exhale.

Squam Lake *(right)*
HOLDERNESS, NH

For those desiring a more peaceful approach to exploring New Hampshire's Squam Lakes region, there are a variety of self-propelled methods to choose from. With its serene beauty, combined with the soft call of loons, it's easy to understand why Squam Lake was the chosen location for the filming of *On Golden Pond*.

NEW HAMPSHIRE 43

Strawbery Banke Museum *(top)*
PORTSMOUTH, NH

Strawbery Banke Museum preserves American history with authentic period homes, shops, and gardens across the ten-acre site. Exhibits and activities, along with costumed reenactors, tell the story of what daily life was like in colonial times. This unique outdoor history museum is on the National Register of Historic Places.

Peterboro Diner *(bottom)*
PETERBOROUGH, NH

The lunch-car diner is synonymous with New England character and charm, and the Peterboro Diner is a prime example. Made by the Worchester Dining Car Company, the historic diner, with its unique green and yellow design, was placed in Depot Square in 1950 and has been serving up great fare ever since.

Blair Bridge
CAMPTON, NH

Spanning the Pemigewasset River in Campton, the Blair Bridge was first built in 1829, only to be destroyed by a man who claimed God had instructed him to burn it. Barring no witnesses, he was found not guilty of the crime. Replaced by a covered bridge in 1869, it was rebuilt in 1977.

Contoocook River
PETERBOROUGH, NH

A misty fog emerges as a thin layer of snow and ice rapidly melts from the surface of the Contoocook River in Peterborough. With much of its 71-mile-long span flowing in an uncommon, northerly direction, the river runs from Contoocook Lake in Jaffrey to Concord.

Bump Bridge

CAMPTON, NH

Located on Bump Road and spanning the quiet waters of the Beebe River, the original covered bridge, built in 1877, was referred to as the Webber Bridge. It gradually fell into a state of disrepair and was rebuilt in 1972, in keeping with the traditional Queenpost style. The modest overpass is for passenger cars only.

Mount Washington Hotel *(top)*
BRETTON WOODS, NH

Overlooking the Presidential Range, this majestic hotel was built in 1902 by Pennsylvania Railroad mogul and New Hampshire native, Joseph Stickney. An iconic National Historic Landmark, the luxurious Spanish-Renaissance-styled retreat, visited by U.S. presidents and dignitaries, is an elite vacation destination.

Cog Railway *(bottom)*
MOUNT WASHINGTON, NH

Chugging its way to the highest peak in New England, the Cog Railway has been offering incredible mountain views for nearly 150 years. The three-mile climb boasts the steepest tracks in the country. The railway's history, as well as exhibits of cog-wheel technology, can be seen at the Marshfield Base Station Museum.

Shopping North Conway *(top)*
NORTH CONWAY, NH

Shops along White Mountain Highway in North Conway display their colorful wares on pedestrian-friendly sidewalks. The area is also well known for its outlet shopping venues where tourists and locals alike enjoy the variety and savings found at Settlers' Green Outlet Village and the White Mountain Outlet Shops.

North Conway Railway Station *(bottom)*
NORTH CONWAY, NH

Renowned architect Nathaniel J. Bradlee designed this unique railway station in 1874, and passenger service to and from Boston continued until 1961. It sat idle until it was reopened in 1974 for scenic railway tours of the Mount Washington Valley. Recognized for its unique details, it is now a National Historic Landmark.

NEW HAMPSHIRE 49

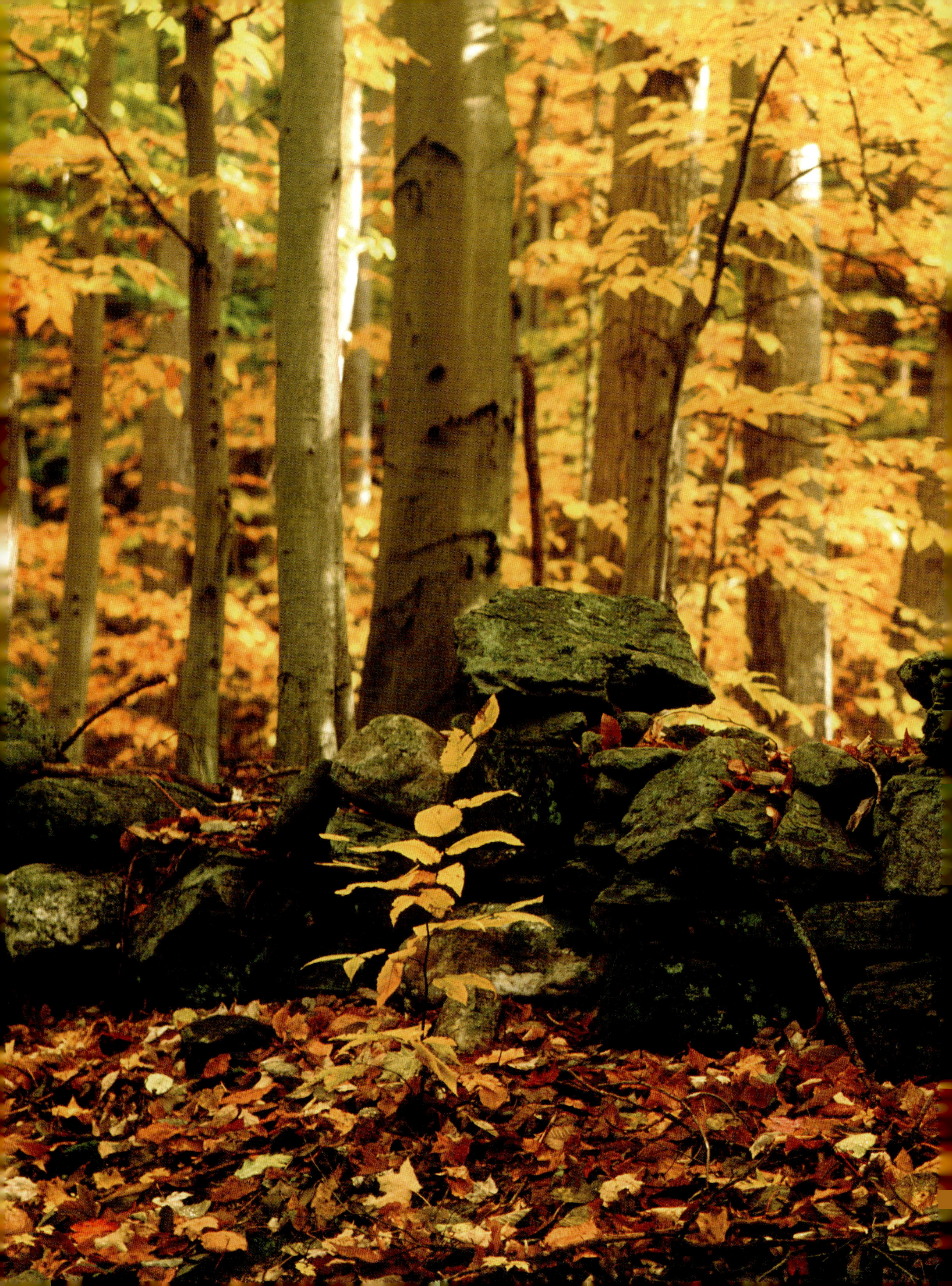

Vermont

The Green Mountain State

RUTLAND, VT

Great Eddy Covered Bridge
WAITSFIELD, VT

Winter sits on a lone bench, patiently awaiting the arrival of spring on the banks of the Mad River in Waitsfield. Spanning the river is a Waitsfield Historic District landmark—the Great Eddy Bridge. Vermont is home to over 100 covered bridges, and the Great Eddy, built in 1833, is the oldest covered bridge in the state.

Vermont State House
MONTPELIER, VT

Built by architect Thomas Silloway in 1857, the Vermont State House, an excellent example of Greek-Revival architecture, was purposely designed to reflect the style of the U.S. Capitol in Washington, D.C. Here, its distinctive high copper dome, covered in gold leaf, gleams against a crisp blue New England sky.

Ben & Jerry's *(above and left)*
WATERBURY, VT

Childhood friends, Ben Cohen and Jerry Greenfield first opened their small ice-cream shop in a renovated gas station in Burlington. Ben & Jerry's is now a household name, and their Ice Cream Factory in Waterbury still produces cool creations with fun names like Cherry Garcia, Chunky Monkey, and Half Baked.

Bennington Battle Monument *(opposite)*
BENNINGTON, VT

Revolutionary War hero Col. Seth Warner is immortalized at the base of a 306-foot-tall monument commemorating the Battle of Bennington, a pivotal Revolutionary War battle fought in 1777. Built in 1891, the monument is the tallest structure in the state, boasting panoramic views of Vermont, Massachusetts, and New York.

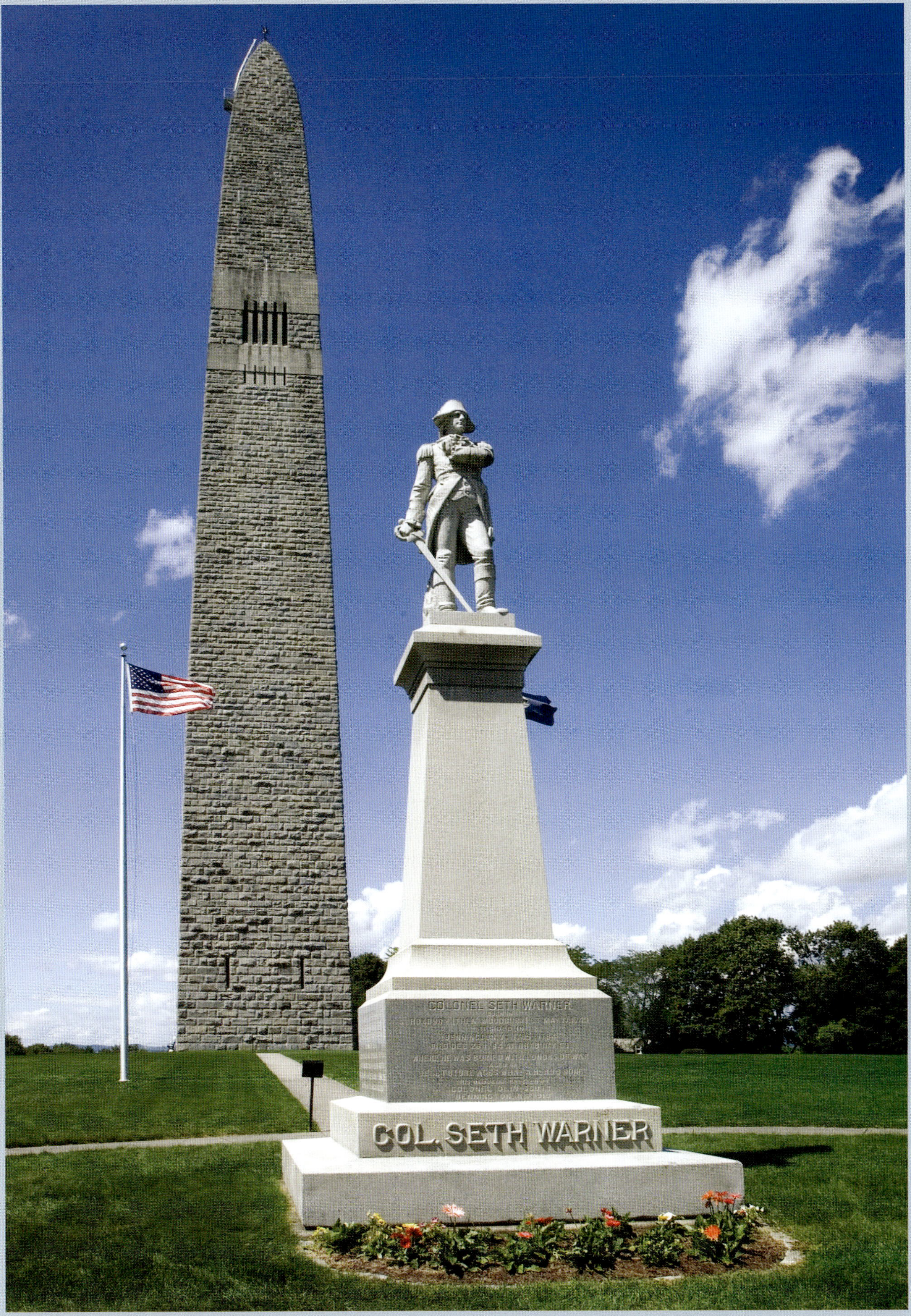
COLONEL SETH WARNER
COL. SETH WARNER

Lincoln Trilogy
BENNINGTON, VT

Sculptor Clyde du Vernet Hunt created *Lincoln Trilogy* in 1939, combining three separate figures into one piece. The three figures—a seated woman, a child, and President Lincoln—represent faith, hope, and charity respectively. Originally named *The American Spirit*, the 9-foot-tall bronze sculpture is located at the Bennington Museum.

Bennington Museum
BENNINGTON, VT

The Bennington Museum has an extensive collection of paintings, toys, furniture, and military artifacts. First founded as the Bennington Historical Association in 1852, today, its permanent collection includes the oldest existing "stars and stripes" and the largest collection of paintings by Vermont folk artist, Grandma Moses.

VERMONT 57

Lake Champlain *(top)*
BURLINGTON, VT

Flanked by the Green Mountains of Vermont and the Adirondack Mountains of New York, Lake Champlain offers incredible scenic boating experiences. Founded by explorer Samuel de Champlain in 1609, the 125-mile-long, fresh-water lake played an important role in American history due to its location and connecting waterways.

Vermont Teddy Bear Company *(bottom)*
SHELBURNE, VT

Classic and cuddly Vermont Teddy Bears have been spreading pure joy since 1981. The Shelburne factory produces adorable bears for an array of occasions and themed bears representing occupations from nurses to firemen to custom-made bears created with personalized details of your choice. Factory tours are available year round.

Burlington Breakwater
BURLINGTON, VT

At the entrance to Burlington Harbor are two small square pyramidal towers. First built in 1857, the wooden structures fared poorly during harsh winters and were eventually replaced using steel frames. Since they are not the original towers, only the breakwater itself is on the National Register of Historic Places.

Maple Sugar Season *(above)*
MORETOWN, VT

Early spring marks the beginning of Vermont's sugaring season. During March and April, trees are tapped to collect the sap that will eventually yield the sweet delicacy that flows over pancakes and enhances recipes everywhere. It takes nearly 40 gallons of maple tree sap to make just 1 gallon of pure delicious maple syrup.

Moretown Farm *(opposite, top)*
MORETOWN, VT

Farmers in the Mad River Valley region produce some of the freshest vegetables, fruits, flowers, and dairy in New England. Some working farms have even become popular vacation venues where learning about the agriculture of where our food comes from is a fun and rewarding educational experience.

Hildene *(opposite, bottom)*
MANCHESTER, VT

This stunning Georgian Revival mansion was the summer home of Robert Todd Lincoln, the eldest child of Mary Todd and Abraham Lincoln. Built in 1905, the 500-acre estate includes formal gardens, an agricultural center, walking trails, an observatory, and more. Guided and self-guided tours are available year round.

VERMONT 61

62 VERMONT

Equinox Resort & Spa *(opposite, top)*
MANCHESTER, VT

Beginning as the Marsh Tavern in 1769, the history of the Equinox has spanned two centuries and includes visits from dignitaries and U.S. presidents. Today, the inn includes 195 rooms in four distinct buildings and offers amenities such as a signature spa, an 18-hole golf course, fly fishing, and challenging off-roading.

Ethan Allen Homestead *(opposite, bottom and above)*
BURLINGTON, VT

Vermont founder and American patriot Ethan Allan built this modest house near the Winooski River in 1787. The outspoken Allan was a farmer and writer, but was best known for the capture of Fort Ticonderoga during the Revolutionary War. The homestead is a living museum where early colonial America comes to life.

Autumn Harvest *(top and bottom)*
RUTLAND, VT

Warm days and cool nights of autumn mean harvest time is here in Vermont. A bounty of corn, apples, pumpkins, and more, along with brilliantly colorful fall foliage, usher in harvest festivals where warm cider, fresh apple pie, and lively music draw locals and tourists alike to celebrations throughout the state.

Glen Moss Falls *(opposite)*
GRANVILLE, VT

From approximately two miles into the Green Mountain National Forest, Deer Hollow Brook empties over varied levels of rock to form a spectacular 35-foot-tall veil of cascading water. One of the most picturesque waterfalls in Vermont, Glen Moss Falls can be easily accessed along Route 100 in Granville.

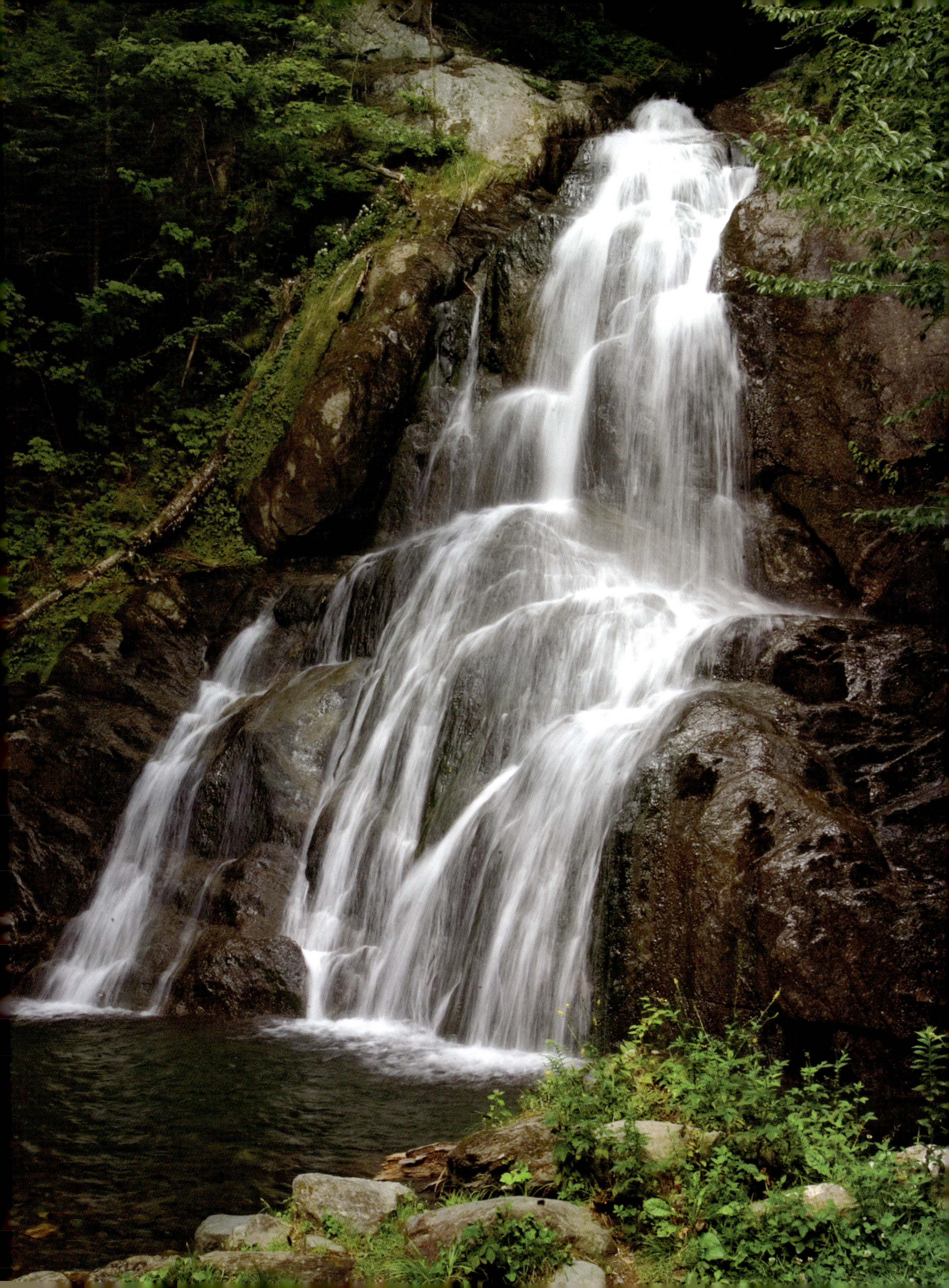

Shelburne Museum Round Barn
SHELBURNE, VT

Built in 1901, the unique Round Barn, with its 80-foot diameter, is a special-exhibit gallery at the Shelburne Museum. Popular in the late 18th century, round barns were considered to be more efficient for the farming methods of that time. Originally built in East Passumpsic, it was moved to its present location in 1985.

Ticonderoga *(top)*
SHELBURNE, VT

The steamboat *Ticonderoga* transported passengers, livestock, and dry goods on Lake Champlain until the early 1950s. A National Historic Landmark, the 220-foot vessel has since been restored and is now part of the Shelburne Museum. The *Ticonderoga* is the last remaining walking beam side-wheel steamer in the country.

Bennington Center for the Arts *(bottom)*
BENNINGTON, VT

A fanciful moose greets visitors of the Bennington Center for the Arts. Founded in 1994 by Bruce Laumeister and Elizabeth Small, the center includes several art galleries with an extensive collection of Native American art, a covered bridge museum, workshop spaces, and a theater featuring world-class performances.

VERMONT 67

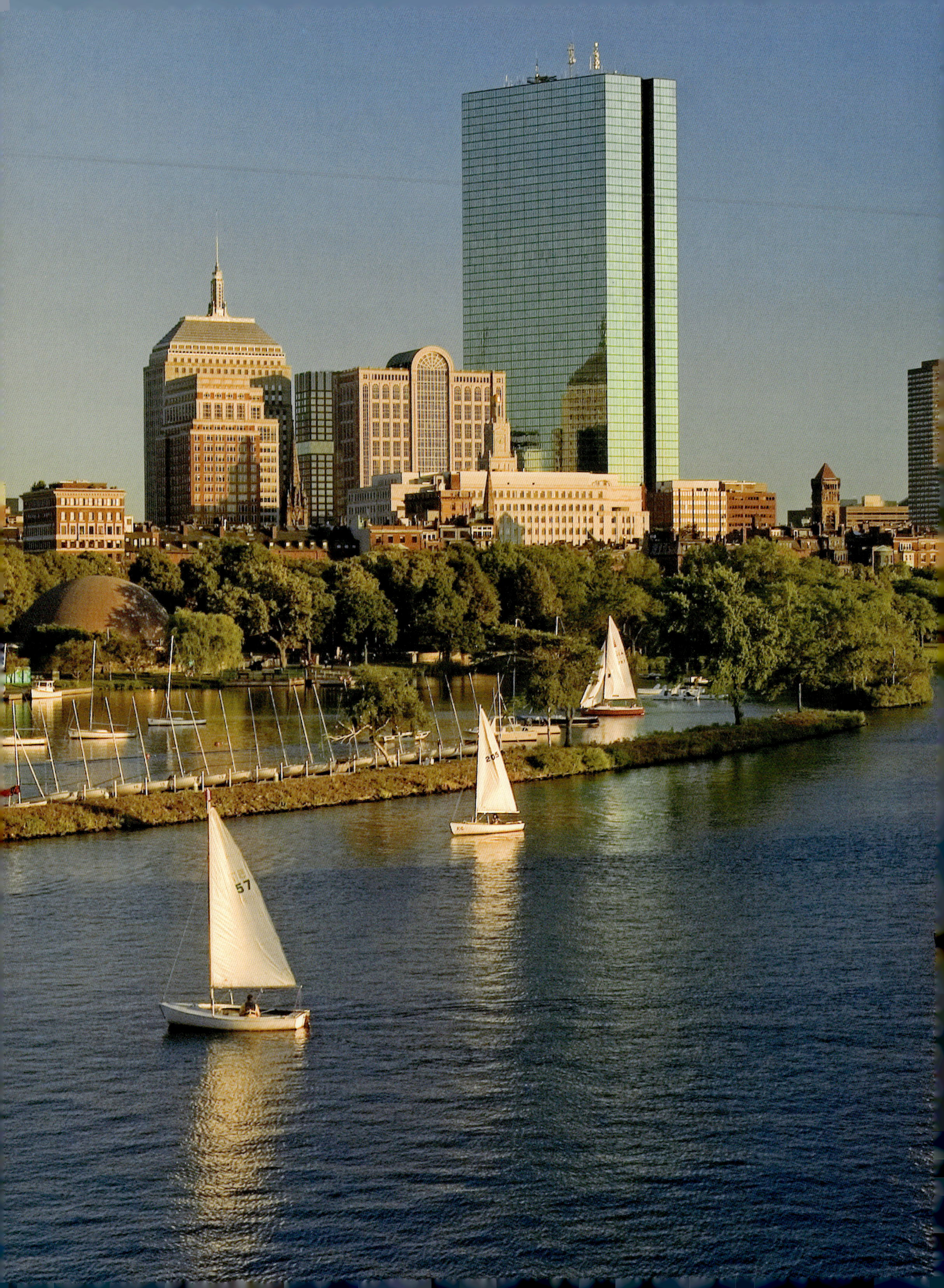

Massachusetts

The Bay State

CHARLES RIVER, BOSTON, MA

Massachusetts State House *(above)*
BOSTON, MA

Designed in 1798 by renowned architect, Charles Bulfinch, the Massachusetts State House is one of the oldest buildings in Boston's Beacon Hill neighborhood. Overlooking Boston Common, the building's gleaming, 23-karat-gold dome is topped with a pine cone, a symbol of the city's 18th-century logging industry.

Faneuil Hall *(opposite)*
BOSTON, MA

Redcoat reenactors stand at the ready at Boston's Faneuil Hall. Gifted in 1742 by Peter Faneuil, the building, dubbed the "Cradle of Liberty," was the location of the first meetings protesting "taxation without representation," and other British policies. Today, it hosts a variety of shops, restaurants, and street performers.

MASSACHUSETTS 71

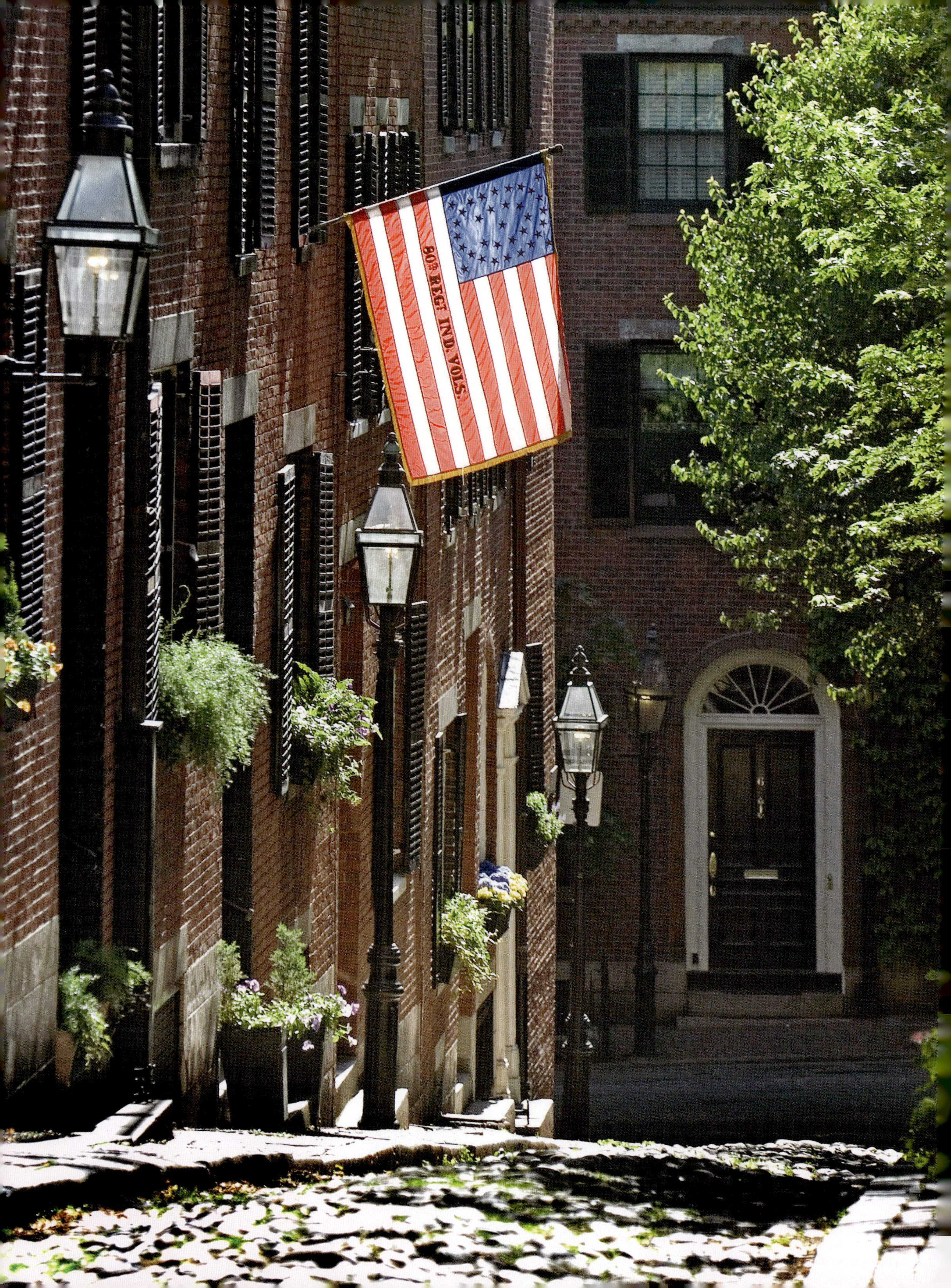
60th REGT IND. VOLS.

Acorn Street (opposite)
BOSTON, MA

Historic Acorn Street, located in Boston's Beacon Hill neighborhood, is one of the last remaining cobblestone streets of its kind. Just one block long and lined with Federalist-styled rowhouses, the small byway was established in the 1820s and is considered one of the most photographed streets in the country.

Boston Public Garden (top)
BOSTON, MA

A pedal-powered Swan Boat gracefully glides passengers along the lagoon in the Boston Public Garden, as has been done each summer since 1877. Part of the Emerald Necklace, the Public Garden, established in 1837, features a variety of finely trimmed hedges, ornamental trees, and seasonal plantings.

Make Way for Ducklings (bottom)
BOSTON, MA

Sculptor Nancy Schön created what has become a beloved Boston landmark in 1987 for the 150th anniversary of the Public Garden. The bronze piece brings to life the 1941 children's story of a mother duck and her ducklings who are guided to the safety of their home in the Public Garden lagoon by a friendly police officer.

HarborWalk
BOSTON, MA

Pedestrians can enjoy a number of parks, seating areas with beautiful views, public art, and more along Boston's 46.9-mile HarborWalk. A result of the revitalization of the waterfront area that was planned in 1984, the walkway meanders along the city's waterfront from Chelsea Creek to the Neponset River.

Rose Fitzgerald Kennedy Greenway
BOSTON, MA

The dismantling of Boston's old, rusting expressway gave way to an expansive green space that now connects the city to its waterfront—a result of the "Big Dig" Central Artery project. The area of small parks and gardens, named for the matriarch of the Kennedy family, has contributed much to the revitalization of the area.

MASSACHUSETTS 75

USS Constitution *(above and left)*
CHARLESTOWN, MA

Launched in 1797, America's oldest warship was built in the city of Boston. The USS *Constitution* was one of six vessels that made up the U.S. Navy. The historic ship is dubbed "Old Ironsides" for the toughness of her oak sides that were left undamaged by British cannonballs fired from the frigate HMS *Guerriere* in 1812.

Minuteman Statue *(opposite)*
CONCORD, MA

In 1875, Daniel Chester French created this tribute to the colonies' first line of resistance at the start of the American Revolution. Located at the Old North Bridge in Concord, *Minuteman* embodies their bravery and determination while encountering British soldiers who were intent on capturing patriots John Adams and John Hancock, and destroying the Minutemen's stockpile of arms.

MASSACHUSETTS 77

Fisherman's Memorial (left)
GLOUCESTER, MA

Gazing steadily toward Gloucester Harbor and beyond, *Man at the Wheel* was created in 1925 by renowned sculptor Leonard Craske. The enduring figure epitomizes the courage and strength of the thousands of mariners who lost their lives at sea. It has fittingly become synonymous with the city of Gloucester.

Double Parked (right)
GLOUCESTER, MA

Brightly colored dories await their next adventurous excursion along the Gloucester waterfront. Whether out for a leisurely sightseeing row, or taking part in the Blackburn Challenge—a grueling, 20+-mile open water race around Cape Ann—taking in the scenic beauty by boat is a delightfully common occurrence.

Rockport Harbor (opposite)
ROCKPORT, MA

Boats moored in Rockport Harbor create an artist's composition, with the famous Motif #1 as a backdrop. The little red fishing shack was rebuilt after the original was destroyed in the Great Blizzard of 1978. It was given the name "Motif #1" by artist Lester Hornby because it was the premier subject matter local artists chose to paint.

78 MASSACHUSETTS

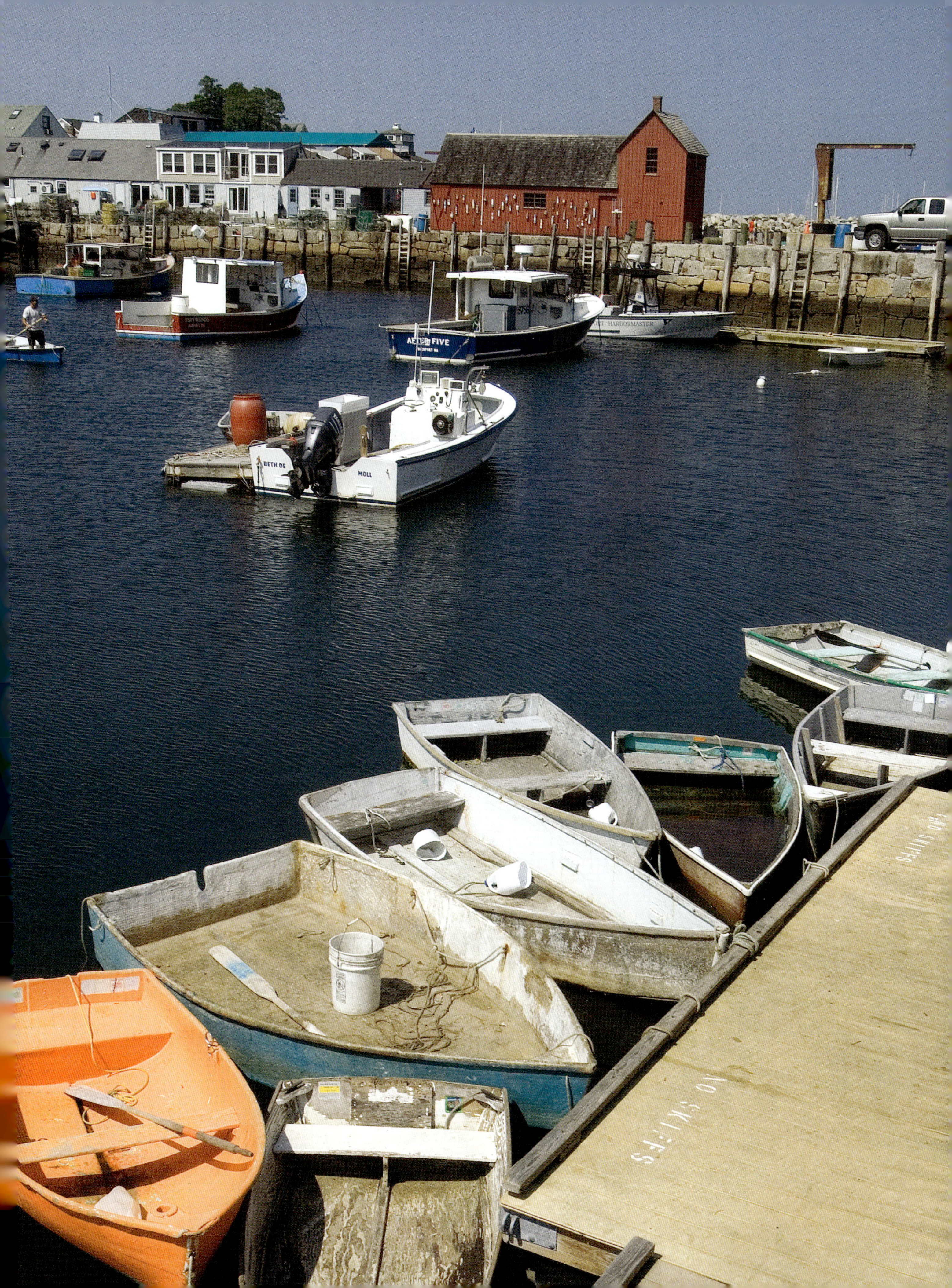
BETH DE
MOLL
HARBORMASTER
NO SKIFFS

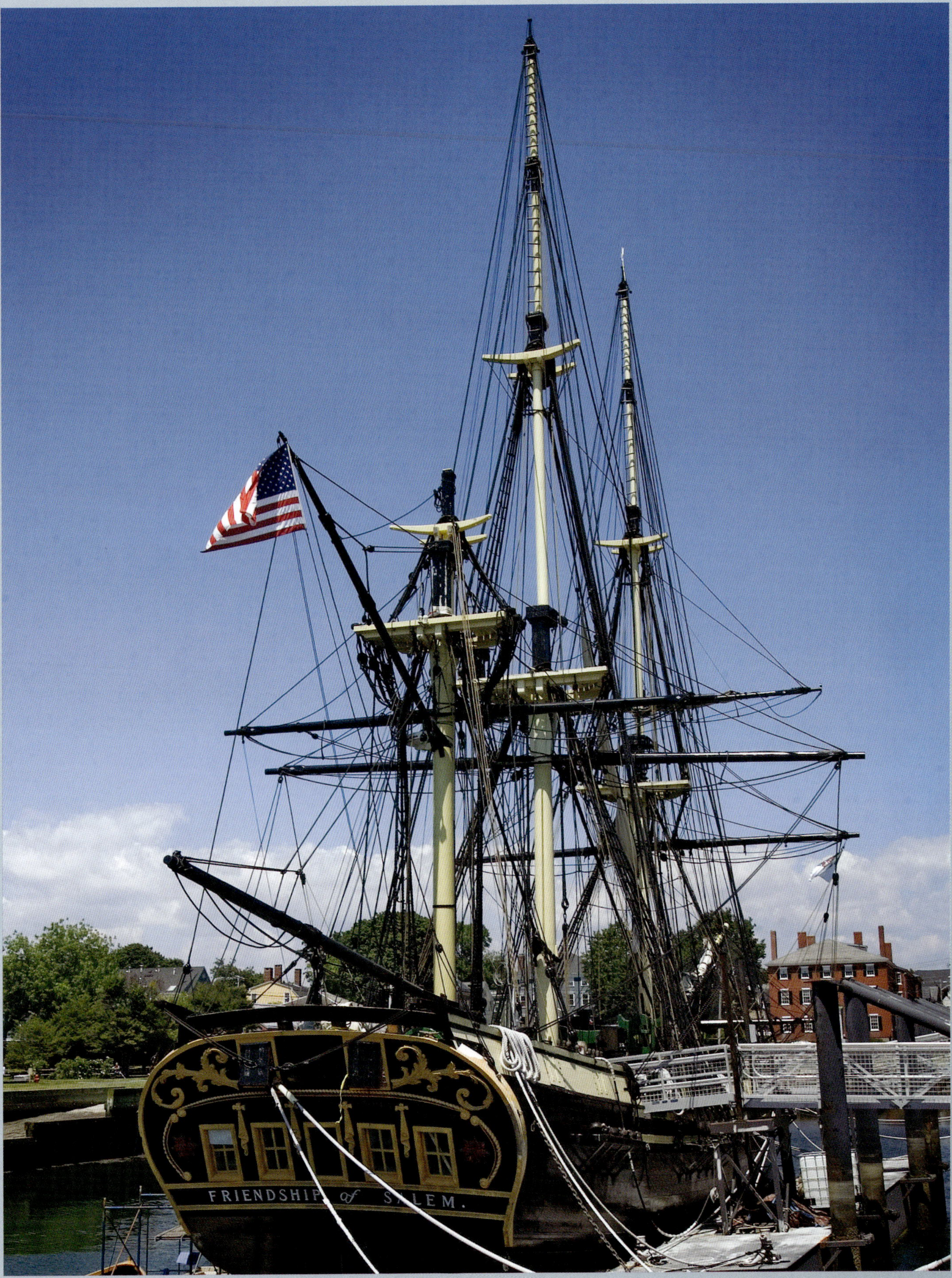
FRIENDSHIP of SALEM.

Friendship of Salem (opposite)
SALEM, MA

Docked at the Salem Maritime Historic Site, the *Friendship of Salem* is a full-sized replica of a 1797 East Indiaman. Built by the Scarano Brothers Shipyard in Albany, New York, the three-masted, 171-foot-long vessel is Coast Guard Certified and sets sail several times a year. Public tours are offered year round, weather permitting.

House of Seven Gables (top)
SALEM, MA

Built in 1668, the House of Seven Gables is the oldest surviving 17th-century wooden mansion in New England. Built by Salem sea captain John Turner, the seaside home is now a National Historic Site, featuring Colonial Revival gardens, art, artifacts, and rare books that preserve over 300 years of Salem's history.

Salem Harbor (bottom)
SALEM, MA

What was once a major international seaport in early colonial America, Salem Harbor is now lined with trendy shops, restaurants, and upscale condominiums. Whether arriving by foot or moored at one of the many yacht clubs or marinas, the Salem waterfront is a popular stop when visiting this incredible historic town.

Historic Seaport *(top)*
NEW BEDFORD, MA

One of the most famous recreational and commercial seaports is historic New Bedford Harbor in southeastern Massachusetts. During the mid-19th century, at the height of the whaling industry era, New Bedford had over 300 whaling ships—more than all other American ports combined.

Heritage Park *(bottom)*
FALL RIVER, MA

The battleship USS *Massachusetts* and destroyer USS *Joseph P. Kennedy, Jr.* are two of five ships deemed National Historic Landmarks located in Battleship Cove at Heritage Park in Fall River. Heritage Park is an 8.5-acre park overlooking the cove and features sailing programs, festivals, and summer concerts.

Scenic Shoreline Village (above)
PROVINCETOWN, MA

The Provincetown Public Library quietly dominates a small-town skyline. Originally home to the former Provincetown Heritage Museum, the library opened in this new location in 2005. It still houses the museum's collection including a half-scale replica of the 66-foot schooner, *Rose Dorothea*.

Pilgrim Monument (right)
PROVINCETOWN, MA

Dedicated in 1910, the 252-foot-tall Pilgrim Monument commemorates the 1620 landing of the Pilgrims in Provincetown. The long climb to the top of the tallest granite tower in the United States is well worth the trek—the reward is a stunning, 360-degree view of Cape Cod Bay and the Atlantic Ocean.

Cranberry Harvest

CARVER, MA

A quiet bog turns into a sea of deep crimson as cranberries float on its surface during the "wet harvest" part of the growing season. First introduced to the Pilgrims by Native Americans, the cranberry is the official fruit of the State of Massachusetts as well as its number one agricultural commodity.

Back Roads (top)
CONWAY, MA

From the coastline to the inland hills, scenic beauty is found throughout the Bay State. Here, along one of many winding back roads, a green pasture gently rolls toward a picturesque barn. Massachusetts farms produce an abundance of fresh goods such as vegetables, dairy products, organic herbs, and seasonal flowers.

Norman Rockwell Studio (bottom)
STOCKBRIDGE, MA

The studio of one of America's most renowned painters is part of the Norman Rockwell Museum in Stockbridge. Rockwell illustrated hundreds of covers for the *Saturday Evening Post*, as well as iconic paintings such as the series *Four Freedoms*. The artist recruited many of his neighbors to pose as models for his works.

MASSACHUSETTS 85

Brant Point Light (above)
NANTUCKET, MA

Located at the entrance to Nantucket Harbor, the original Brant Point Light was built in 1746. Since that time, 10 different versions of the beacon have occupied the point—some lost to fire; others to harsh winter weather conditions. The current picturesque, 26-foot-tall tower with its footbridge was established in 1901.

Summer Island Retreat (left and opposite)
MARTHA'S VINEYARD, MA

A trio searches for sea life in front of the historic Edgartown Light (opposite) on the island of Martha's Vineyard. Summer breezes and timeless New England charm of towns such as Oak Bluffs (left) beckon vacationers and summer residents to return to the island each year. A seven-mile ferry ride from the mainland, the Vineyard boasts some of the best beaches, sailing, biking, golf, and dining in the region.

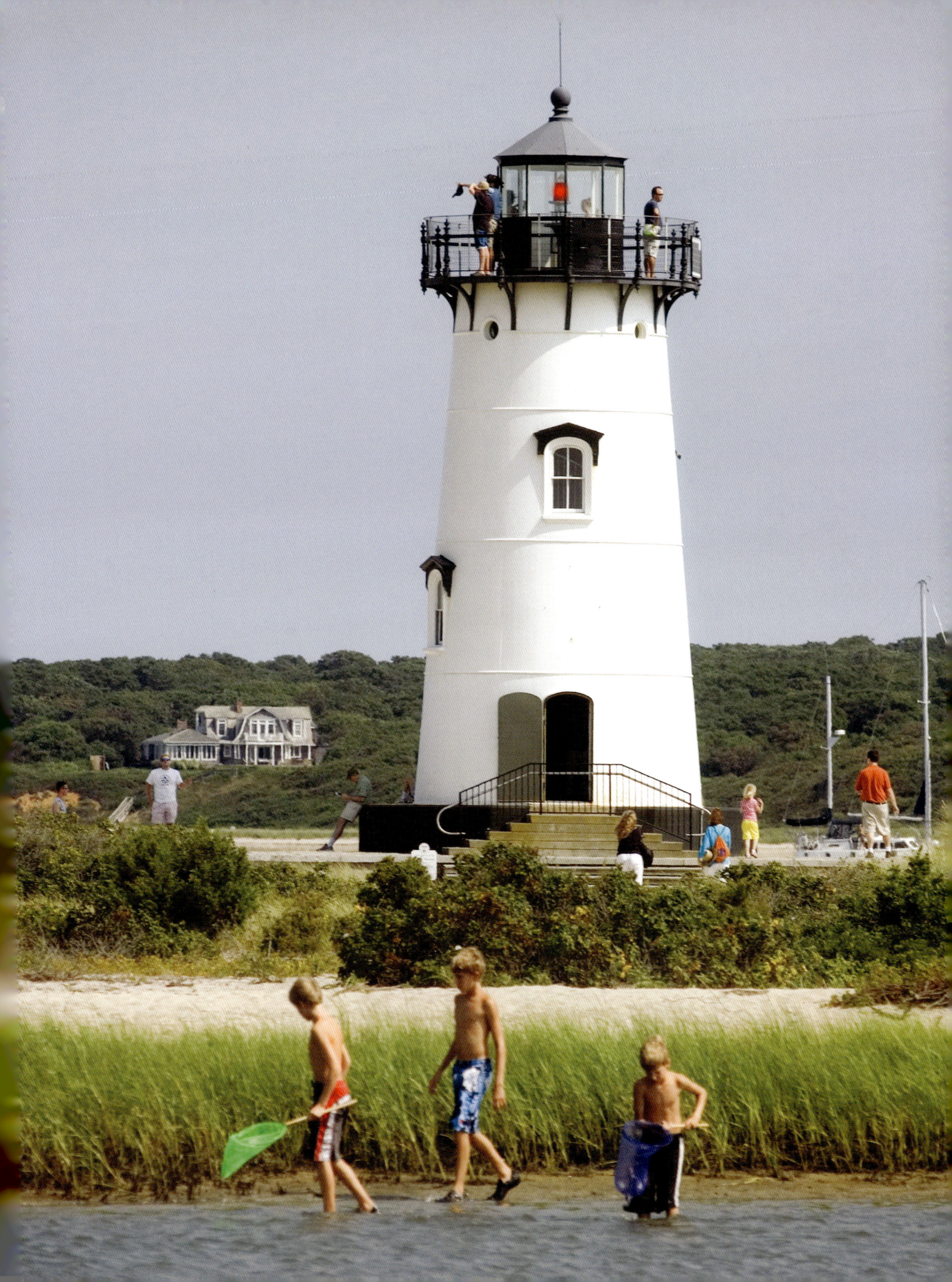

Chatham Light (top)
CHATHAM, MA

Due to a long history of shipwrecks, a lighthouse station comprised of two towers was first established at the bend of Cape Cod's "elbow" in 1808 to help guide mariners around the Cape's extremely treacherous waters. The 80-foot-tall Chatham Light still stands and remains an active Coast Guard Station today.

Nauset Light Beach (bottom)
EASTHAM, MA

The Cape Cod National Seashore is 40 miles of incredible scenic beauty along the entire outer coastline of the Cape. At its southern end, in Eastham, is Nauset Light Beach, a spectacular beach with dramatic dunes that face the Atlantic Ocean. This historic spot was also home to a late 19th-century transatlantic cable station.

Mayflower II *(above)*
PLYMOUTH, MA

At 106-feet-long and only 25-feet wide, this full-scale replica of the *Mayflower* is owned by Plymoth Plantation and docked in Plymouth Harbor. Reproduced in great detail, visitors can board the *Mayflower II* and experience what a transatlantic journey would have been like on a 17th-century ship.

Plymouth Rock *(right)*
PLYMOUTH, MA

Plymouth Rock Monument in Pilgrim Memorial State Park marks the landing place where William Bradford and the Pilgrims first disembarked from the *Mayflower* in 1620. Nearly one million people visit the iconic boulder each year, although there is no official account of the Pilgrims actually stepping onto a rock.

English Village *(above)*
PLYMOUTH, MA

History comes to life at Plimoth Plantation, a living museum where reenactors re-create 17th-century Colonial life. Daily chores, including tending gardens, the upkeep of houses, and caring for livestock, are all part of depicting the harsh realities that the first American colonists had to face in order to survive.

Wampanoag Homesite *(left)*
PLYMOUTH, MA

A Native staff member uses fire to hollow out a tree that will become a seaworthy canoe. Plimoth Plantation's Wampanoag Homesite, along the Eel River, depicts the daily lives of the Wampanoag people as they go about their chores, tending fields of tobacco and corn, making baskets, and building homes.

Plimoth Plantation
PLYMOUTH, MA

Wood-framed, thatch-roofed homes paint a vivid picture of what life was like in a small farming and maritime community in 1627. At Plimoth Plantation, colonial role-players dressed in period costume, reveal captivating stories, each from their own individual point of view of life in a 17th-century English village.

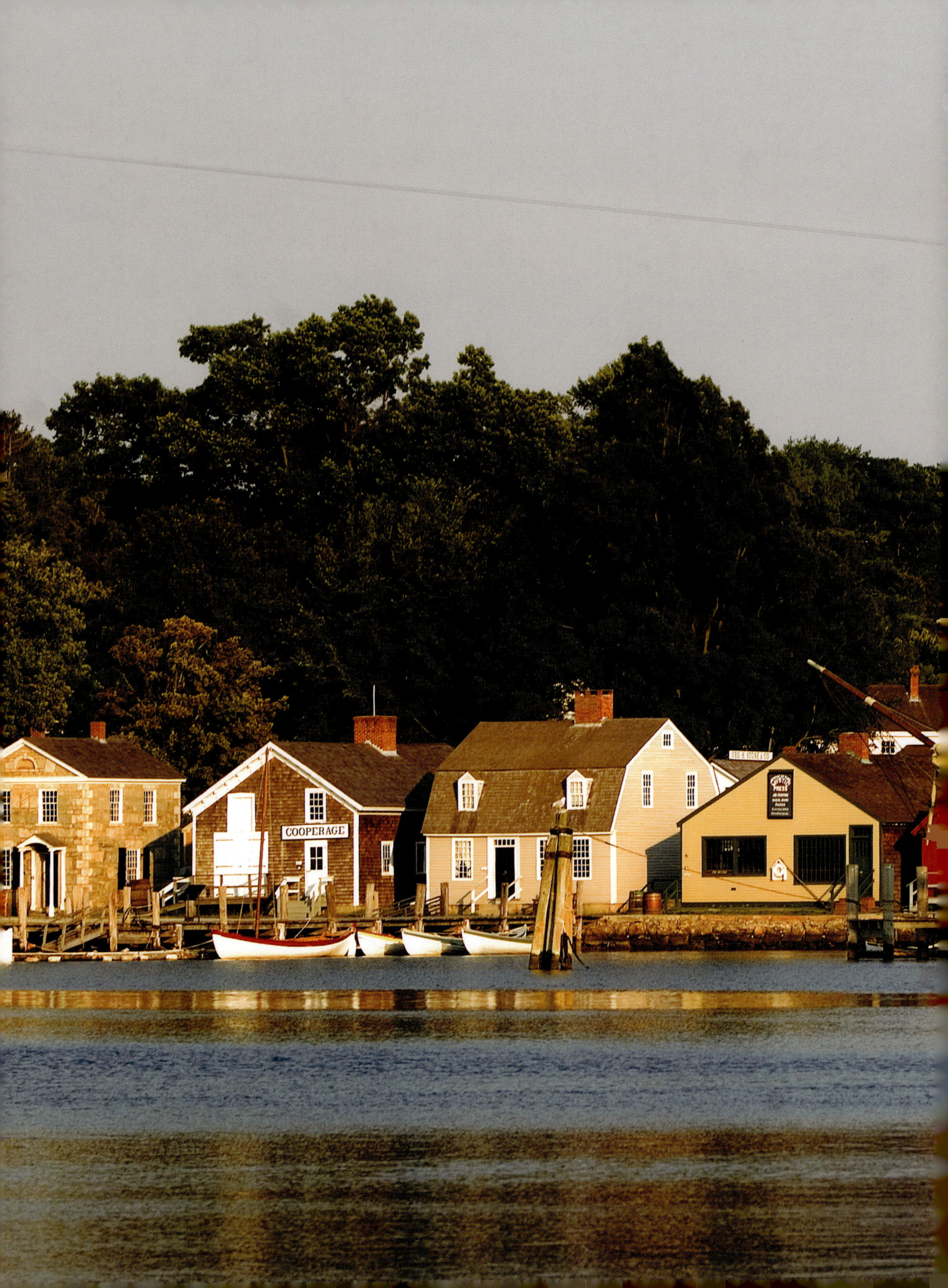
COOPERAGE

Connecticut

The Constitution State

MYSTIC SEAPORT, MYSTIC, CT

Connecticut State Capitol *(above)*
HARTFORD, CT

Located in Bushnell Park, Connecticut's Victorian Gothic-styled statehouse fittingly has the ambience of an elegant church. It was designed in 1878 by Richard M. Upjohn, a cathedral architect. The building is home to executive offices as well as historical state artifacts.

Hartford City Hall *(left)*
HARTFORD, CT

One of the most beautiful buildings in Connecticut's capital city, Hartford City Hall opened in 1915. The Beaux-Art-styled building is faced with Bethel white granite and features stunning bronze entrances. It is listed on the National Register of Historic Places.

Connecticut River Museum *(opposite)*
ESSEX, CT

The Connecticut River contributed greatly to the establishment and growth of many New England regions. The Connecticut River Museum preserves the heritage of the river through educational programs, guided tours, river cruises aboard the schooner *Mary E*, and more.

CONNECTICUT 95

Roseland Cottage
WOODSTOCK, CT

With its colorful exterior and manicured gardens, Roseland Cottage was the summer home of businessman Henry Bowen and his family. Also known as "The Pink House," the 1846 Greek Revival-styled cottage is located on over 60 acres of land on Roseland Lake. The building and grounds are open to the public.

Harmony (above)
HARTFORD, CT

Aptly named *Harmony*, this graceful modern sculpture is in tune with the flow of Bushnell Park Pond, its elegant fountains, and surrounding greenery. Dedicated in September of 1990, the stainless steel piece is the work of native Connecticut sculptor Charles Perry.

Soldiers & Sailors Memorial Arch (right)
HARTFORD, CT

The gateway to Bushnell Park, the arch is a memorial to the thousands of Hartford citizens who served in the Civil War. The Gothic brownstone structure, designed by architect George Keller in 1886, includes Civil War scenes and depictions of various Hartford residents, from farmers to students, who contributed to the war effort.

Corning Fountain *(above)*
HARTFORD, CT

A noble stag stands atop the 30-foot-tall *Corning Fountain* in Bushnell Park. Designed by James Massey Rhind, the fountain features Saukiog Indians who were the first inhabitants of Hartford. Corning Glass Works founder, John Corning, presented the fountain in 1899 in honor of his father.

Bushnell Park Carousel *(left)*
HARTFORD, CT

The magnificent vintage 1914 carousel in Bushnell Park features a thunderous Wurlitzer band organ, two chariots, and 48 wooden horses, hand carved by Russian immigrants and craftsmen, Solomon Stein and Harry Goldstein. It is one of only three remaining Stein and Goldstein carousels in existence today.

Captain Nathaniel B. Palmer House
STONINGTON, CT

With panoramic views of Stonington Harbor from the octagonal cupola, this Victorian mansion was built in 1852 by Captains Nathaniel Brown Palmer and Alexander Smith Palmer. The brothers built the 16-room residence high on "Pine Point" so their families could view ships arriving and departing the harbor.

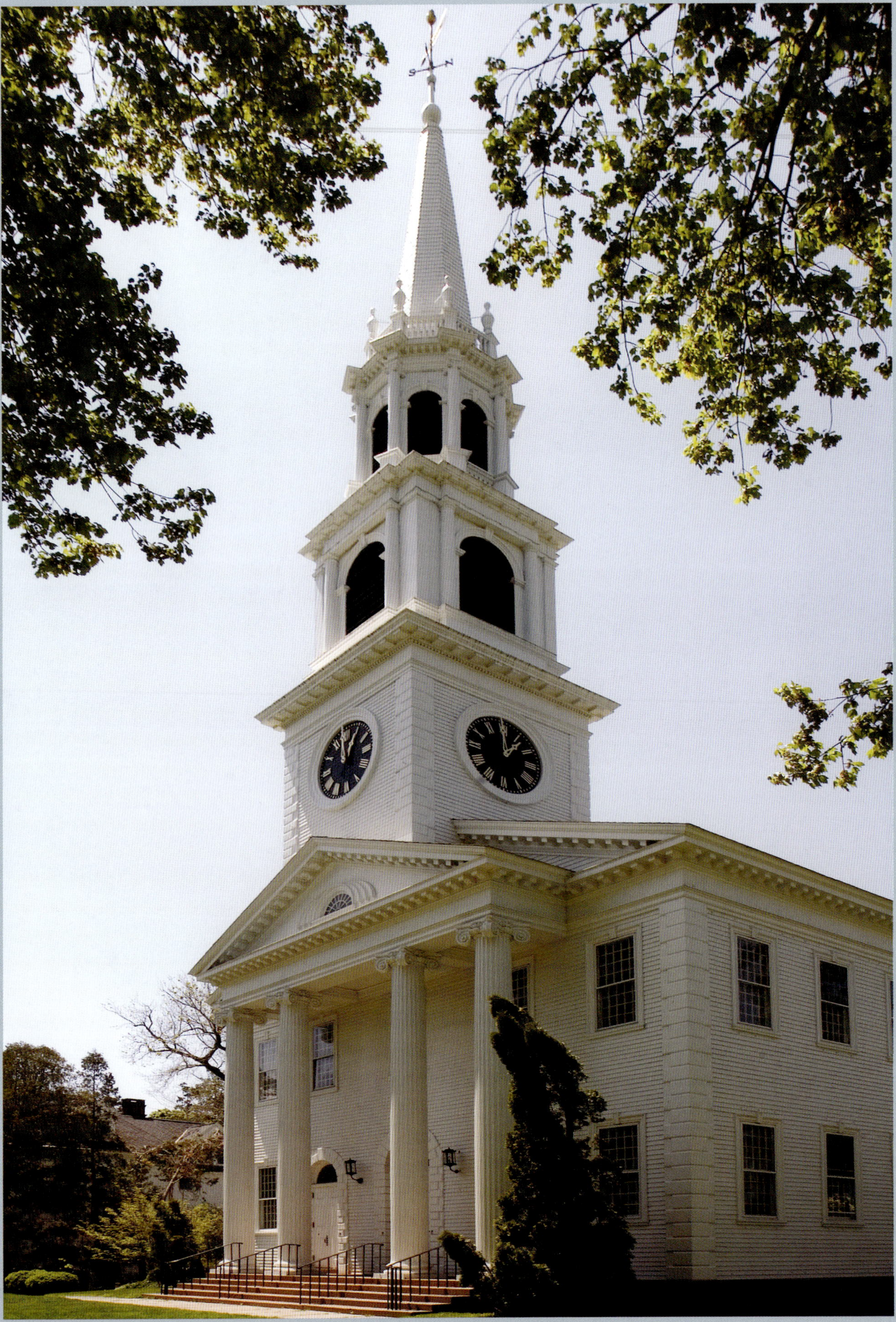

First Congregational Church *(opposite)*
OLD LYME, CT

An Old Lyme landmark, the First Congregational Church was originally built in 1816, and rebuilt after it was destroyed by a mysterious fire in 1907. With its historical significance and simplistic beauty, it has been the subject of many famous paintings, including those of renowned American Impressionist Childe Hassam.

War of 1812 Monument *(top)*
STONINGTON, CT

Two great guns flank an obelisk in Cannon Square commemorating the battle for Stonington during the War of 1812, when a group of five British warships attacked the city for four days in 1814. The monument lists the names of ten residents who manned the massive cannons and successfully fought off the British Naval forces.

Griswold Inn *(bottom)*
ESSEX, CT

Used as a base of operations by British soldiers during the War of 1812, the historic Griswold Inn has been providing lodging for more than 234 years and is one of the oldest continuously run taverns in the U.S. With its picturesque Essex Village setting, the "Gris" is a popular venue for weddings and special events.

Harriet Beecher Stowe House *(above)*
HARTFORD, CT

Built in 1871, this classic 14-room New England home was the residence of American author, Harriet Beecher Stowe, who penned *Uncle Tom's Cabin*. The home is where most of her later works were written. Located along the Connecticut Freedom Trail, tours of the historic home and gardens are available year round.

Florence Griswold House *(opposite, top)*
OLD LYME, CT

Florence Griswold opened her home to boarders in the late 1890s for financial reasons. It became an ideal setting for artists and eventually the home to the Lyme Art Colony, a group of notable American Impressionist painters. The home is part of the Griswold Museum, which includes galleries, learning centers, and gardens.

The Cooley Gallery *(opposite, bottom)*
OLD LYME, CT

Adding to the friendly ambience of the bright yellow building, a poised amphibian artfully greets visitors to The Cooley Gallery in Old Lyme. Open Tuesday through Saturday, the gallery has an extensive collection of American paintings, sculpture, photography, crafts, jewelry, and antiques.

CONNECTICUT 103

Mark Twain House (top)
HARTFORD, CT

Renowned American author Samuel Clemens (a.k.a Mark Twain) spent some of the most productive years of his life in this splendid Hartford home with his wife and family. Built in 1874, the Victorian mansion includes a conservatory, billiard room, and library where the author would often tell stories to his family and friends.

Essex Steam Train & Riverboat (bottom)
ESSEX, CT

From picturesque countrysides of quaint New England towns, to unspoiled inlets and coves, the Essex Steam Train & Riverboat is a great way to experience the beauty of the Connecticut River Valley. The journey begins aboard a vintage steam locomotive and culminates with a riverboat cruise along the Connecticut River.

Yale University
NEW HAVEN, CT

Founded in 1701, this prestigious Ivy League university has a long history of firsts including the first planned college campus, the first college art museum, and the first college newspaper. Accomplished alumni with degrees from Yale University include several U.S. Presidents, Nobel laureates, and Pulitzer Prize winners.

Lighthouse Point Park (top and opposite)
NEW HAVEN, CT

The 82-acre park along beautiful Long Island Sound features swimming, fishing, and nature trails as well as the historic Five Mile Point Lighthouse. Built in 1847 and named for its distance to downtown New Haven, the 65-foot-tall, octagonal tower is listed on the National Register of Historic Places.

Gillette Castle (bottom)
EAST HADDAM, CT

Formerly the residence of American actor William Gillette, famous for portraying Sherlock Holmes, this 1914 medieval castle is now part of a 184-acre state park. Named *Seventh Sister* for the hills it was built upon, the castle's intriguing interior includes extraordinary features such as hidden mirrors and a disappearing bar.

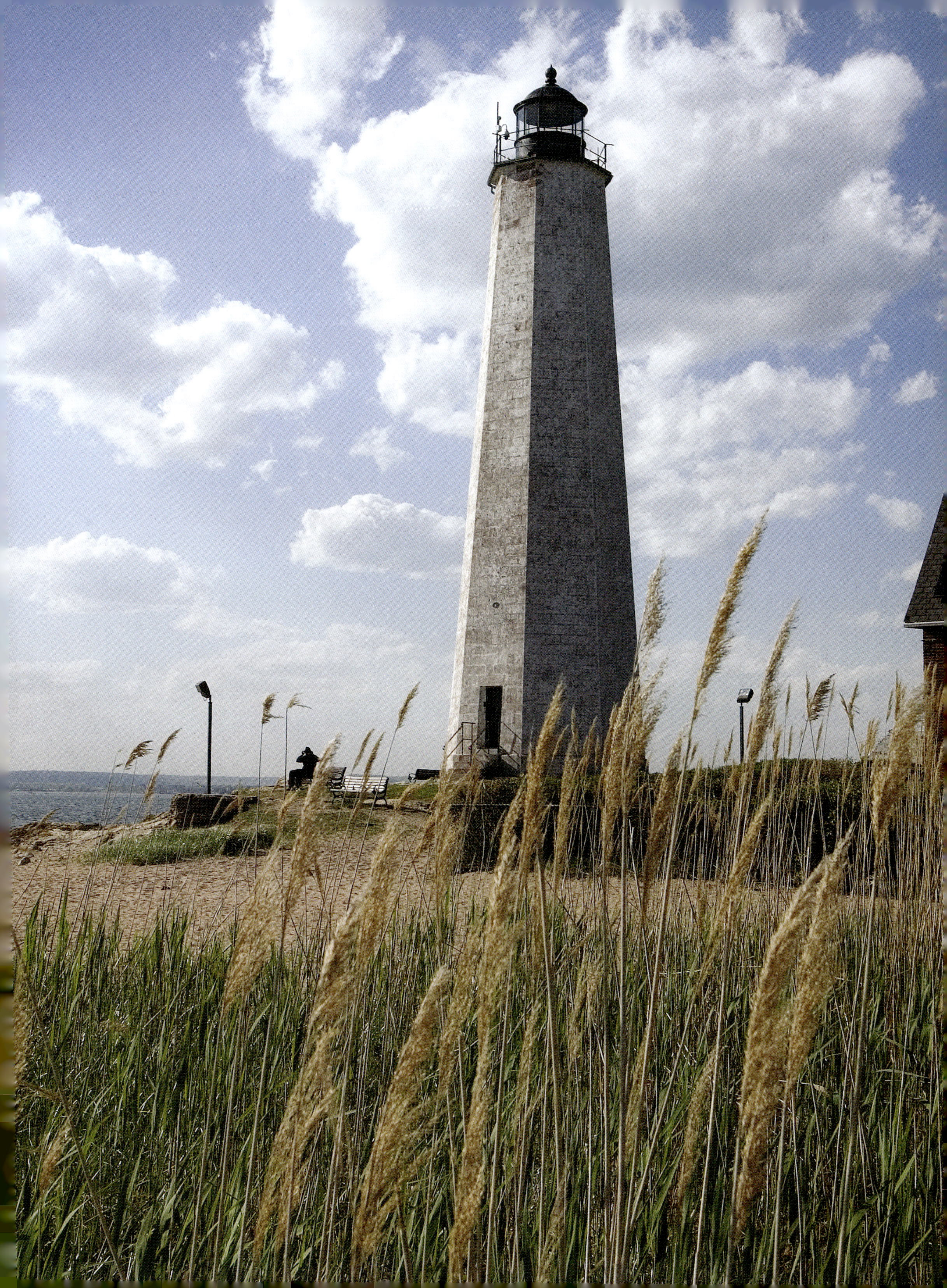

Mystic Seaport *(top)*
MYSTIC, CT

Enthusiasts of seafaring history step back in time to this 19th-century New England village that is part of the Mystic Seaport Museum of America and the Sea. Also included are an extensive collection of art and artifacts, historic vessels, demonstrations, sailing programs, summer camps, and multi-level learning programs.

Mystic River Drawbridge *(bottom)*
MYSTIC, CT

Passengers aboard a sightseeing schooner glide beneath the historic Mystic River Drawbridge. Designed in 1920 by the Chief Engineer of Otis Elevator Company, the *bascule* bridge (derived from the French term for *balance scale*) opens every hour, as well as on demand, totaling approximately 2,200 openings per year.

Old Lighthouse Museum *(opposite)*
STONINGTON, CT

Unique for its decorative granite stonework, this stalwart tower marks the entrance to Stonington Harbor. Built in 1840, the light had guided vessels safely across Fishers Island Sound for over 170 years. Acquired by the Stonington Historical Society in 1925, today it houses a variety of centuries-old maritime artifacts.

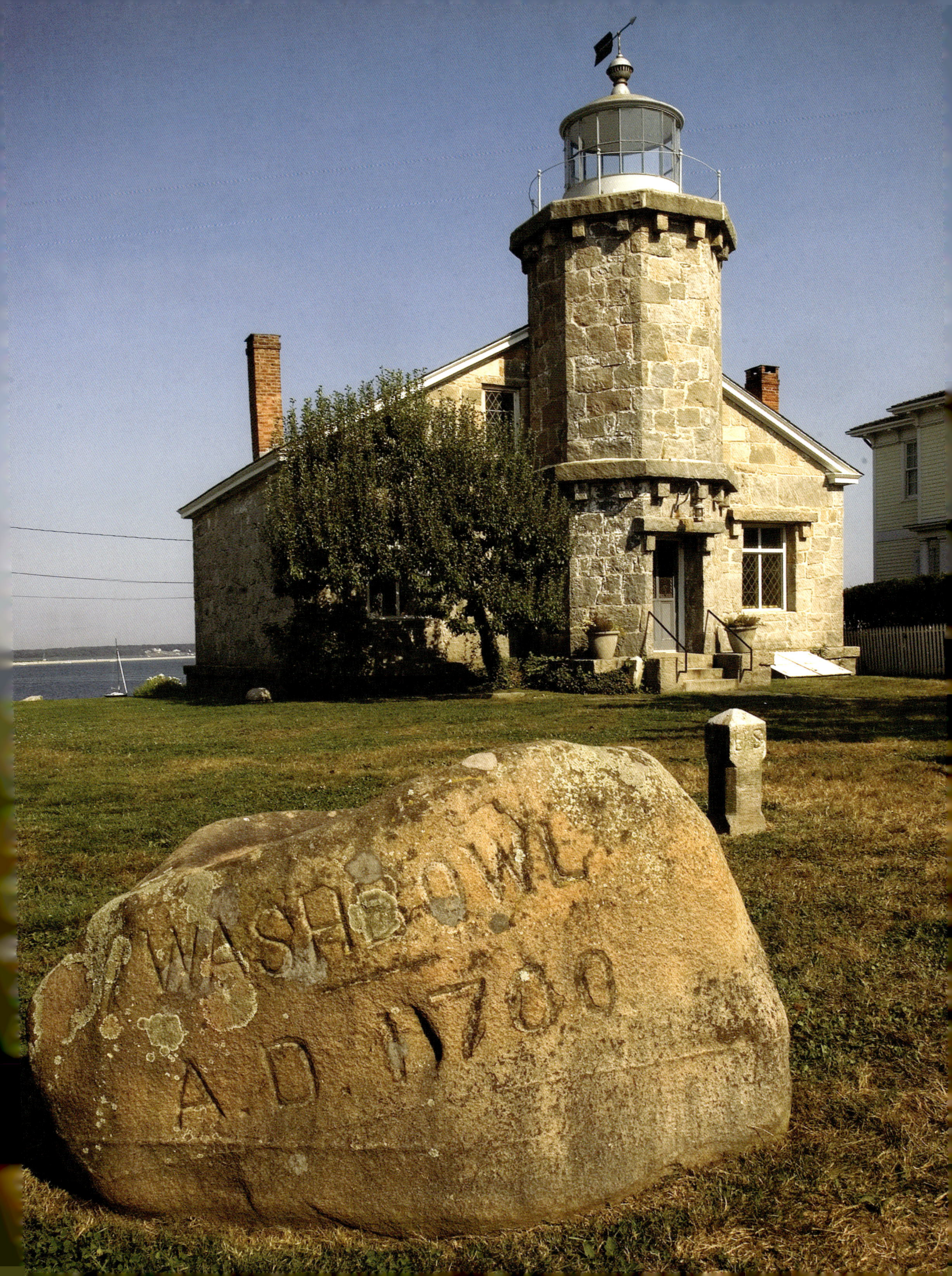
WASH OWL
A.D. 1700

110 CONNECTICUT

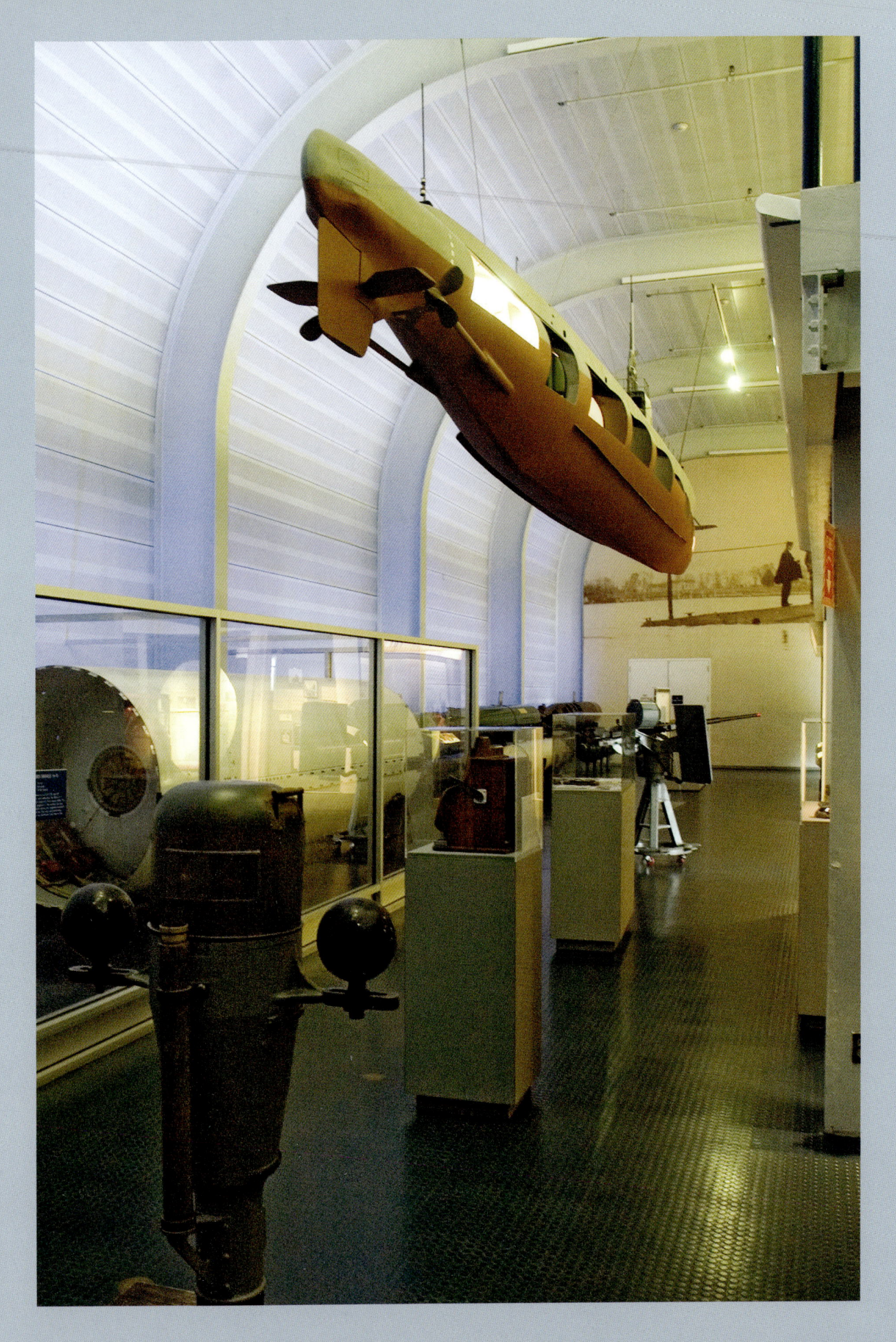

Submarine Force Museum *(opposite and top)*
GROTON, CT

Delve into U.S. submarine history with more than 80,000 artifacts, photographs, and documents at the Submarine Force Museum located on the Thames River in Groton. Managed by the United States Navy, the museum boasts the finest collection of submarine artifacts in the world as well as an extensive research library.

USS Nautilus *(bottom)*
GROTON, CT

First launched in 1954, the USS *Nautilus* was the world's first nuclear-powered submarine. Decommissioned in 1980, the vessel is now part of the Submarine Force Museum where visitors can explore her torpedo room, galley, attack center and more, for an "in-depth" understanding of day-to-day undersea life of a submariner.

CONNECTICUT 111

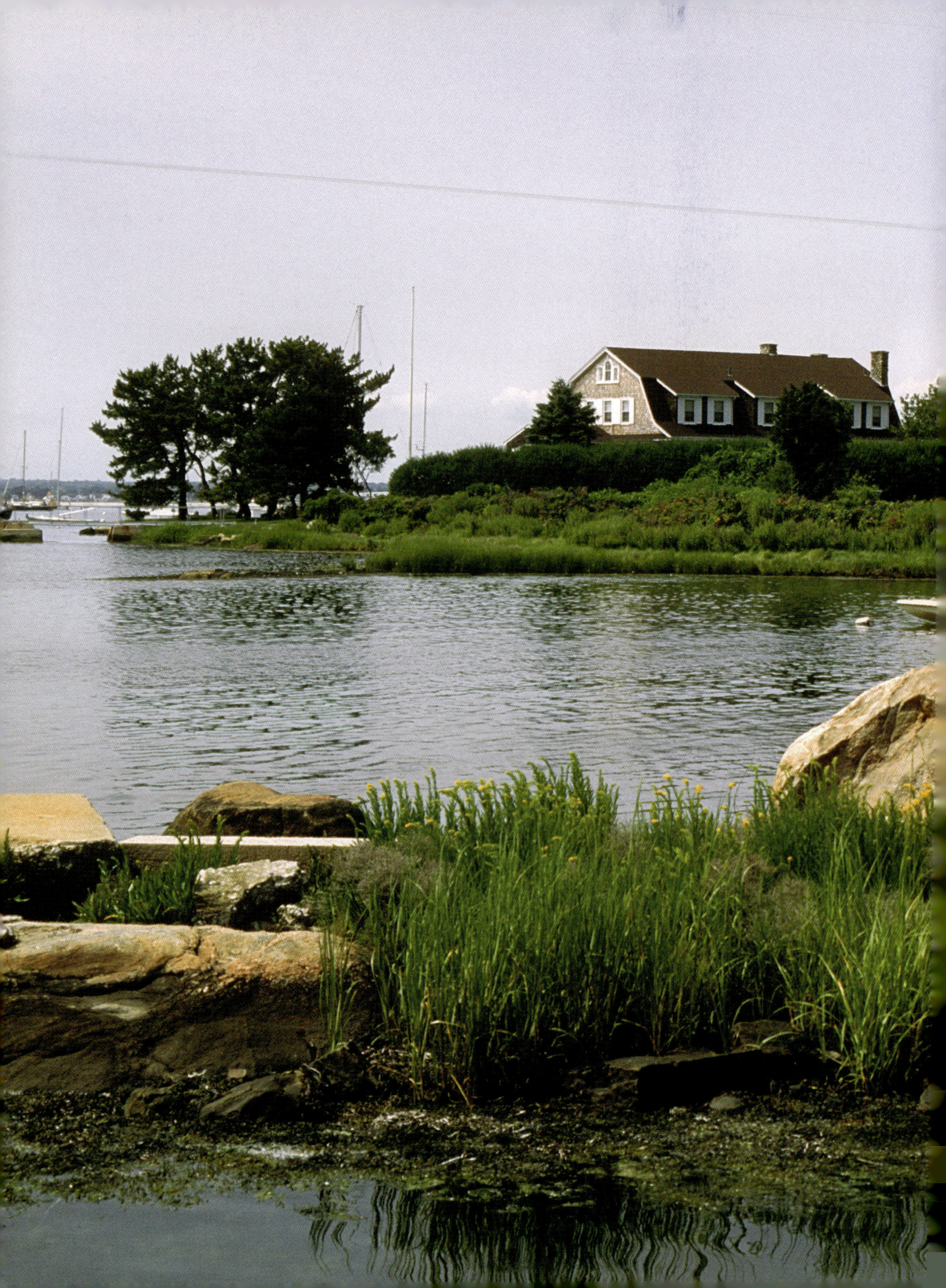

Rhode Island

The Ocean State

WESTERLY, RI

114   RHODE ISLAND

Castle Hill Light (opposite)
NEWPORT, RI

Built directly into a cliff, this rugged, 34-foot-tall tower, located at the East Passage of Narragansett Bay, has guided ships through thick fog and inclement weather since 1890. Closed to the public, the lighthouse site, with its spectacular views, can be accessed via a trail on the grounds of the Castle Hill Inn and Resort.

Aquidneck (top)
NEWPORT, RI

What better way to experience the beauty of the "sailing capital of the world" than aboard a magnificent schooner. The 80-foot-long *Aquidneck* cruises through Newport Harbor and along the Rhode Island coastline offering views of colonial homes and luxurious estates, lighthouses, historic sites, and more.

Old Slater Mill (bottom)
PAWTUCKET, RI

The roots of America's Industrial Revolution are well grounded in New England. Built in 1793, Old Slater Mill was the nation's first factory, producing thread and, over the years, everything from cardboard to bicycles. The National Historic Landmark is now a museum preserving the rich history of American innovation.

Rose Island Lighthouse (top)
NEWPORT, RI

Easily identified by its unique mansard roof, the historic 1870 lighthouse, located on the 18.5-acre Rose Island, is operated by the Rose Island Lighthouse Foundation. Accessible by ferry, visitors can enjoy a daytrip, or experience the life of a lighthouse keeper with a memorable overnight stay in the "keepers" quarters.

Conimicut Lighthouse (bottom)
WARWICK, RI

Conimicut Light was built on the shoal off Conimicut Point in 1868. Keepers of the 58-foot-tall tower had an interesting and tragic past, from the survival of Horace Arnold at the destruction of his quarters by floating ice in 1874, to the suicide of Ellsworth Smith's wife as she succumbed to the unbearable isolation in 1922.

Cliff Walk *(top)*
NEWPORT, RI

Along the Atlantic coastline in Newport is a 3.5-mile path that meanders along cliffs and rocky shorelines, offering commanding views of the ocean as well as glimpses of the formal gardens and embellished gates of Newport's famous waterfront mansions. Cliff Walk was designated a National Recreation Trail in 1975.

Prescott Farm *(bottom)*
MIDDLETOWN, RI

A 19th-century windmill ushers in spring breezes at Prescott Farm. This 40-acre farm is dedicated to the preservation of historic buildings starting with the Nichols-Overing House (c. 1730) and featuring the Robert Sherman Windmill, the Hicks House, the Sweet-Anthony House, and the Guard House among others.

Congdon Street Homes *(top)*
PROVIDENCE, RI

Well-maintained historic homes stand at attention along Congdon Street, a tree-lined thoroughfare that runs through Providence's desirable College Hill neighborhood. From Greek-revival to Georgian-style, urban renewal projects during the 1950s helped to restore much of the area's 17th- and 18th-century architecture.

Watch Hill Gazebo *(left)*
WATCH HILL, RI

The view from the gazebo that overlooks Watch Hill Harbor is serene in any kind of weather. Watch Hill is a small coastal New England village situated on a peninsula that is almost entirely surrounded by the Atlantic Ocean. The gazebo is a wonderful spot for intimate wedding ceremonies or persnickety day dreamers.

Newport Waterfront

NEWPORT, RI

Whether taking in the skyline view from the bow of an elegant sailboat or exploring the seaside boutiques and restaurants, Newport's waterfront is a unique combination of vibrancy and history contained in a plethora of scenic beauty. Drawn by its charm and excellent seafood, crowds flock to the town known as New England's summer resort.

The Breakers *(top)*
NEWPORT, RI

Home to Cornelius Vanderbilt II, President of the New York Central Railroad, The Breakers is one of Newport's most impressive waterfront estates. Designed in 1893 by architect Richard Morris Hunt, this Italian Renaissance "summer cottage" includes 70 rooms. The National Historic Landmark is open to the public.

Rosecliff Mansion *(bottom)*
NEWPORT, RI

Built in 1902 in the style of the Grand Trianon, a royal garden retreat in Versailles, Roscliff was the estate home of silver heiress, Theresa Fair Oelrichs. The mansion hosted some of Newport's most lavish parties in the early 20th century and was the location where many of the scenes from *The Great Gatsby* were filmed.

Waterfire *(opposite, top and bottom)*
PROVIDENCE, RI

Dozens of flickering bonfires installed on the three rivers of downtown Providence comprise *Waterfire*, a stunning and inspiring work of art by sculptor Barnaby Evans. The sculpture is lit several times a year, drawing thousands to Waterplace Park and contributing to much of the revitalization of downtown Providence.

RHODE ISLAND 121

Old Commons Burial Ground *(top)*
LITTLE COMPTON, RI

There are over 50 historic cemeteries in the town of Little Compton, some, the burial grounds of the nation's first Pilgrims who arrived on the *Mayflower*. One such is Elizabeth Alden Pabodie, eldest daughter of John Alden and Priscilla Mullins, who is buried here in the Old Commons Burial Ground in Little Compton Commons.

Carolyn's Sakonnet Vineyard *(bottom)*
LITTLE COMPTON, RI

With conditions closely resembling those of the great wine regions of northern France, Carolyn's Sakonnet Vineyard produces award-winning wines. Established in 1975, the vineyard, located on 115 acres, also offers an exquisite venue, complete with breathtaking water views.

International Tennis Hall of Fame *(opposite)*
NEWPORT, RI

The International Tennis Hall of Fame & Museum, located in the historic Newport Casino, includes an inspirational collection of historic art, attire, equipment, and more. The Hall of Fame honors champions of bygone eras as well as contemporary legends such as John McEnroe, Martina Navratilova, and Pete Sampras.

RHODE ISLAND 123

Gilbert Stuart Birthplace & Museum
SAUNDERSTOWN, RI

Born in the room above his father's snuff mill in 1755, the nation's most significant portrait painter, Gilbert Stuart, captured the essence of Presidents, Revolutionary War heroes, and prominent people of 18th-century America. His most recognized piece is the unfinished portrait of George Washington that appears on the dollar bill.

Coggeshall Farm Museum
BRISTOL, RI

A living museum set on 48 acres depicts agrarian life in late 18th-century America. Roleplayers in period costumes perform the chores of the time, enlightening visitors to the day-to-day challenges these first farmers had to endure. Established in 1973, the museum provides an exceptional learning environment.

Roger Williams Park Bandstand *(top)*
PROVIDENCE, RI

The current bandstand in Roger Williams Park is an exact replica of the original that was designed by architect John Hutchins Cady in 1915. Its retro design evokes bygone days when music from the bandstand filled the soft summer air. With its location on Roosevelt Lake, it is often the perfect setting for wedding ceremonies.

Roger Williams Park and Zoo *(bottom)*
PROVIDENCE, RI

Children of all ages delight in the train ride at the Roger Williams Park and Zoo. Founded in 1872, it is one of the oldest zoos in the U.S. The zoo not only features more than 100 fascinating species of animals, it is also the region's top center for environmental education, offering programs for both adults and children.

Botanical Center *(top)*
PROVIDENCE, RI

Fragrant flowers from all around the globe envelop visitors at the Roger Williams Park Botanical Center. Comprising nearly 12,000 square feet, it is the largest indoor garden in New England. Conservatory and attached greenhouses along with relaxing water features make this the perfect urban oasis.

Roger Williams Park Carousel *(bottom)*
PROVIDENCE, RI

A memorable trip to Roger Williams Park would undoubtedly include a visit to Carousel Village. Children can ride a camel, giraffe, or seahorse on the Victorian-styled, covered carousel or discover endless fun at Hasbro's Boundless Playground. Stop by the gift shop for a treasured keepsake of the visit.

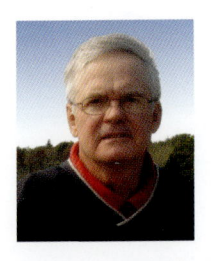

Tom Croke has more than 50 years of experience in the field of photography, particularly in the areas of high tech, advertising illustration, portrait, studio/location, journalism and sports/action photography. He worked as the manager and chief corporate photographer with The New England in Boston, Massachusetts, and as the manager of photographic services for The Foxboro Company, Foxborough, Massachusetts where he designed and managed a large studio and lab operation in addition to performing corporate advertising assignments. He was the team photographer for The New England Patriots from 1975 through the 1991 seasons and an official NFL photographer from 1975 through the 2001 seasons until the NFL decided to dissolve their library. He now markets his work through ICON Sports Media.

For the past 25 years, Tom and his wife, Anna, have co-owned Visual Image, Inc., in Dennis, Massachusetts. Established in 1987, Visual Image, Inc. is a communications concern specializing in advertising, public relations, commercial, editorial and fine art photography - the majority of their work being location photography. Please visit their website: www.visualimageinc.com to view their latest work produced for their many clients over the past 20 years of business including the NFL, ICON Sports Media, New England Psychology, Condyne, LLC, Bridgewater State University and Twin Lights Publishers.

Award-winning graphic designer, Sara Day, has always been inspired by the beauty of New England. A native of Gloucester, Massachusetts, Sara has enjoyed a long career working with publishers, photographers, and advertising agencies. She uses her talents to create exquisite photo journals as well as promotional materials. To see more of her work, visit www.sypdesign.com and www.twinlightspub.com.